Learning Elephant

Use the Power
of
Applied Feelings
Intelligence

Walt Froloff

Published by
patentAlchemy Press,
Aptos, Ca

Editor: Joan Rose Staffen
Cover Illustrations: Joan Rose Staffen
Cover by Leslie Torvik

Dedication

I wish to dedicate this book to Joan. Had she not come forward, enthusiastically encouraged me, and volunteered to edit and direct me on this project this book would not have happened. The art illustration is her creation, spawned by feelings. Simply put, without Joan this book would not be.

Guest House

This being human is a guest house.
Every morning a new arrival.
A joy, a depression, a meanness,
some momentary awareness comes
as an unexpected visitor.
Welcome and entertain all!
Even if they're a crowd of sorrows,
who violently sweep your house
empty of its furniture,
Still, treat each guest honorably.
He may be clearing you out
for some new delight.
The dark thought, the shame, the malice,
meet them at the door laughing,
and invite them in.
Be grateful for whoever comes,
because each has been sent
as a guide from beyond.

Rumi – 13th Century

TABLE of CONTENTS

Preface

You Are More Intelligent Than You Think

Like you always knew from deep within - you are much smarter than you think. If you have ever felt that you know many secrets that cannot be accessed or that you are more than you are, that there is a part inside of you that is not being used or used very well, then you have brushed up against your feelings intelligence. To tap into your feelings intelligence, you must first learn the language of emotions. Then find out all the amazing things you have been trying to tell yourself through your feelings. Find out why and how you are so much smarter than you think, more powerful than you act, when you tap and leverage the information that you feel.

Although thinking intelligence is all that we have been taught we have, deep down we know that we have more - it's the feeling intelligence. We can use our feelings information to find the edge, use our innate advantage to find solutions, inform our decision-making to better ourselves, and attain our highest potential by working *with* instead of against ourselves.

I am a recovering engineer, and this work evolved from a previous book, *Irrational Intelligence,* which includes my theory of emotions in a format compatible to technologists for the purpose of programming electronic devices. But my theory of emotions is broader, and so that formed the need, purpose, and reason for this work - to offer another answer to why we feel what we feel, when we feel it.

Many have wondered why they have feelings or if their feelings have value; why they feel, what they feel, when they feel it. But who can benefit from feelings intelligence? The curious, the helpless, the hopeless, the powerful and the powerless can benefit. This book will take the mystery out of emotions, just enough to make them useful and you clairvoyant.

Emotions seem to be tied closely with our lives, almost as if they provide purpose and motivation. Indeed they do but I have purposefully avoided the search for our life's purpose. Those issues are well addressed by others. For example, in *Man's Search for Meaning*, Victor Frankl finds that life is not primarily a quest for pleasure, as Freud believed, or a quest for power, as Adler taught, but a quest for meaning.

This book is about the tools we carry on the quest to achieve our purpose, what to do when we enter the forces-beyond-our-control house. We will learn how to tap into and rely on emotions and the reserves inside that arise when we need them least and most.

John Shedd gave us:

> "A ship is safe in the harbor, but that is not what ships were made for."

So grab your hat and travel gear. You are packing for all weather including the doldrums and storms, so that you not only survive them, but learn to enjoy the journey as well.

Introduction

Nature's Gift – Your Wild Elephant

An ancient Indian philosophy held that humans are comprised of three basic components – thinking, feeling, and behaving. To explain how the thinking, feeling and behaving can operate best as one, they imagined the components as three elephants. The emotions were a wild elephant, a part of our being that had abundant energy that needed to be controlled and directed to do useful work. The thinking and behavior components were trained or trainable elephants.

The Indian method of controlling and training a wild elephant was well known and well practiced. Two trained elephants were placed and bound by ropes on each side of the wild elephant to control and steer him. This by analogy is the strategy used for management of human emotions, wherein we control emotions by directing our thinking and behavior, the parts of us that we can control.

Contrary to everything you've been taught, your wild elephant does **not** need to be controlled, manipulated, or trained to be useful. In our haste and error to harness the wild elephant's energy, we have become inhumane to the wild elephant; we have denied all that the wild elephant is. That is, we have denied who we are. In our present understandings and teachings, we have reduced our emotions, their power, and contribution.

Our wild elephant is talking to us, telling us things we need to know about the road up ahead, the steep ravines on the sides, the traps on the road, the distance to camp, the ambush that waits in the jungle or the tranquil teal lagoon just outside of eyeshot. We don't need to fight with or control the wild elephant; we just need to know what the wild elephant is saying.

Using the power of our emotions begins with learning Elephant. Once we understand Elephant, we can lose the ropes of bondage, take the wild, powerful elephant on a full gallop unencumbered, enjoy the ride, and see the sights on the journey, secure in the elephant's strength and wisdom to the path up ahead.

1 – Welcome and Entertain Them All

Feelings are the vital information, the part of us that gives us common sense, reason, inspiration, and creativity. This is most of what makes us unique and human. The present computer cannot accomplish even the simplest examples of common sense, reason, inspiration, or creativity, because a computer feels no pain, knows no pleasure, has no feelings, can't reason and therefore cannot take advantage of all that we take for granted.

We receive this intelligence without thinking, through emotive signals. These provide a summation of our experiential database, our biochemical processes, and current sensory intelligence. This intelligence may be conscious or unconscious, and pertains to a matter that should concern us in the present moment.

Thinking Intelligence vs. Feelings Intelligence

Ever searched for some lost keys? You know what they look like and your eyes are doing mix and match scanning over all of the objects that might look like those keys. Even if it's just your friend's keys, you can help. Your thinking recalls what keys look like. They have physical identifiable characteristics. They look and feel metallic and are shaped like a key with teeth for the lock. You may even recall where you last remember seeing them.

It takes most of our attention, concentration or mental focus to search for something. That is thinking intelligence. We recall from stored memories, identify characteristics, use pattern matching, concentration and deduction.

But what if we were searching for someone or something whose very definition is unknown? With no identifiable parameters, characteristics or attributes. Furthermore, we cannot spend any time-consuming thinking effort searching. But what if it was the just most important thing in our life? OK, let's say we are single and looking for that special someone, our soul mate.

Logically, using our thinking intelligence, we could never find our soul mate. Why? We don't know what they look like. We don't know anything about them. We have no identifiable characteristics. We don't even know what kind of person we can live with harmoniously for a length of time. We don't know what kind of person we want to spend a good part of our life with, except maybe in a very general sense. And we can't spend our time focusing on a search for them because we're busy making a living, spending time our friends, contributing to social groups, eating, sleeping, exercising, staying healthy and more. Our thinking intelligence fails us in our most important pursuits.

But if we were at a business lunch and our soul mate walked in, we would get a feeling, something about them would spark our *interest*. Interest is a feeling that directs our thinking to analyze the interest object further.

There is a stark difference between the two types of intelligences, thinking and feeling. Thinking is a step-by-step, one focused thought at a time sequential process. Feelings are spontaneous and asynchronous. They happen all by themselves, without mental focus and whenever they want. We provide no mental effort to bring our feelings about. Our feelings interrupt our train of thought to inform us that it's time to think about something else, the subject of the feeling.

It is remarkable, that our feelings pop up like popcorn and not only tell us when its time to do some thinking, but what to think about. We are interrupted hundreds of times a day. Though we rarely give our feelings a second thought, they work for us without resting, directing our thoughts this way and that.

We may be working on a business deal, we may be negotiating, taking orders for some product or service. We are thinking and feeling. Feelings inform us about what is happening around us, inside us, and to us. They do this 24/7 and don't require any thinking energy.

Turning back to the example of searching for our soul mate, our interest informed us of their presence. What's next? Thinking intelligence then tells us our best strategy to get them to come over is to smile and say hello.

Then we may feel *curious* about this person. Our thinking intelligence will respond by formulating some questions. Are they dependable? How much money do they make? Do they have a car, what kind?

13

Will they treat us well? Will they *care* about us after sex? Buy us flowers? Take us out for long walks on the beach? In the moonlight or just around the block now and again?

We may find ourselves flooded with a sea of questions that we need answered for a valid identification. We have no idea if they are being truthful. They are free to say anything we want to hear. And we know that if they are "the one," and we ask all those questions, they may likely mumble something like, "Oh I forgot to feed my gerbil," and retreat, as we may have just become too intrusive and thus potentially "high maintenance."

Or ... maybe we will get that feeling of *excitement* when they see us. Our *excitement* is informing us something new and good is about to happen. But as you may have discovered, many guys have a one-item checklist. He comes over and lays down one or more of a dozen lame come-on lines: "Is it warm in here, or are you just hot?"

Then that other feeling hits us, like our stomach is turning. We have felt it before. It's *revulsion*. We didn't even have to ask a question. Our feelings intelligence says, "Turkey, stay away." And our *revulsion* has informed us that we need to create distance from this obviously-not-our-soul mate, because we know further interaction would not turn out well.

On the other hand, he might do something intelligent like come over and say "Hi I'm Ted, What's your name? May I join you? And we might reply something noncommittal like, "Helen. Please do." We may have a conversation during which time we will get a feeling or seven:

- *excitement* or *anticipation* – because they're available
- *connection* – because they're communicative
- *security* - because they're reassuring
- *playfulness* and *joy* - because they're fun
- *romance*, chemistry – because they're sexy
- *relief* – because they have a good stable job
- *comfort* – because they has status, education or culture
- *commonality* – because they have a compatible religion, ethnicity, or common group

Do they make us feel *Safe? Secure? Valued? Respected? Playful? Relaxed? Excited?* That's our feelings intelligence; it just filtered out the losers. We have given ourselves the green light for a date. We didn't have to fill out a questionnaire. The rush of feelings converged and said, "This is more than promising."

Each feeling we receive carries the answer to an important issue that will affect our relationship later. So we can wisely decide presently, something vital to our future. We're applying our feelings intelligence so that our search is successful.

That was easy, life is complicated. We may have experienced a broken relationship in which we invested some time. We know that breakups can be devastating, and very painful. Especially when we ignored our feelings that warned us of the rocky road ahead.

15

If we were *rejected* in the past because we were slightly overweight, now we will test for that up front, to find out whether our physical appearance will be a deal breaker. On future dates, more will be established as to compatibility, companionship, and maybe love. But these will all require feelings intelligence. That is how we find our soul mate.

What They Are, Where They Come From

The ancient Egyptians took all of the internal organs out for mummification, but the heart was put back into its place. They believed that the soul and real intelligence of a man lived in the heart. The heart is after all, the symbolic seat of our emotions, our persona, and our energy source. These are all that we would need in the afterlife, so they put that vital component back so the king could move on in the afterlife. Note that they did not leave the brain in, only the heart. Even then, the ancient Egyptians knew that the real intelligence of a man was in his emotional makeup, heart, not logic.

So what is a feeling? A feeling derives from that perfect sum, a multiplexer operation that converts all relevant experiential and physical information we possess on a matter that confronts us. All of that is jammed into a small entity, the feelings, upon which we can rely for our best decisions. The issue that confronts us may or may not yet be at the conscious level or even confronting us in the present. In fact, much of the time, feelings are anticipatory.

That feeling signal is a mechanism of our survive and thrive imperative, which is stored in our cognitive brain in the feeling register, data-readable through introspection and brought to us by fast massive parallel memory access. That feeling is based on all the information we have inside us and all that we are. It is perfect information and a consolidated truth from us.

The source of that feeling signal is thousands of tributaries inside us: our total memories, plus nine senses, times innumerable biochemicals from hormones, drugs, stimulants, neurotransmitters, and more.

The destination of that feeling is our conscious thinking mind or cognitive brain. Each feeling or emotive state is a separate and distinct signal, accessible through introspection where the feeling intensity is low, or an undeniably inescapable conscious interrupt, if the intensity is high.

From infancy, before language and before logic, we all use a simple learning pattern. Actions elicit an experience that is stored and made accessible through feelings. Since all feelings have degrees of pleasure and pain, we naturally tend to avoid the painful and gravitate toward the pleasurable ones.

But conscious avoidance of feelings skews our awareness and reduces the information received. In order to receive all that the wild elephant is saying, we cannot pick and choose which feelings we will decrypt and which we won't address. We must gratefully receive all our feelings. This is the beginning of feelings intelligence and it is developed early.

A Mere Question Can Cause Pain

I had an experience with my son when he was approximately four years old. We had a pet rat that developed a growth on his long furry snout. My son and I first noticed this puss blister together while observing our pet observing us. Our pet had a somewhat painful look to him, which prompted me to accusingly question my son if he had been poking him with a sharp implement. That started tears rolling down my son's face as he denied the accusation. Even though it was merely a question, he felt a pain in my accusation.

From this I learned that a mere question can cause tremendous pain, and that even a four year old has developed a sharp intelligence beyond logic, beyond knowledge and beyond his years, beyond text, and in advance of formal learning. That a false accusation cuts as deep as a knife. That a question to me seemed necessary enough but to him it was unthinkable, that I would believe him capable of abusing our little pet creature. His feelings towards our pet were true. The thought that I may have inflicted abuse through an improper memory disturbs me even still. The next day, I apologized profusely and we both cried over it.

Our pet eventually died from the tumor and we both grieved the loss, but I remember that day I inflicted great pain with a little question. That painful experience lives within us both and is now part of our life experience. It makes us both wiser as we make judgments and decisions based on our experience continually, without ever having to point to this or that one specific event. Our shallowest to deepest judgments, prejudices and biases are based on our sum total of experiences and knowledge. These are quickly accessed and delivered through our feelings.

Emotions Come in Two Flavors

Today the battle between Negative Psychologists and Positive Psychologists rages on. These are based on "negative" and "positive" emotions. You chose what you will feel by thinking positively or negatively, or by subjecting yourself to positive or negative situations or circumstances. Many teach think positive and you will be happier and healthier by and large. Think negatively and negative circumstances or behavior will arise to make you feel less happy and even bad.

However, emotions only come in two flavors, pleasure and pain, not positive or negative. Positive or negative are artificial distinctions, not natural ones. Together, pain and pleasure provide information and train us to go in the direction we should go, to make the correct decision, to do the right thing in situations and circumstances. Furthermore, the intensity of the feelings tells us how much, how fast, and how important it is to address the feelings messages.

Never an Over Supply

There is never an over supply of feelings and we will never have extra emotions. Nobody is overly emotional. Some of us are more animated or just don't know what to do with all of our emotions. However, if we are not using our emotions, we are wasting time, wasting effort, or wasting life. Emotions are vital because they tell us what to think about and when to think about it.

For the painful emotions, there is a comfort in knowing that within typical settings and normal parameters, the pain level has design limits that we can endure. The benefits bestowed from our painful emotions are easily worth the pain. If the pain becomes greater than we can endure, our body will automatically shut down consciousness. We will blackout until the pain can be reduced. Then we automatically reboot to a conscious state. Moreover, without the pain, we would not know pleasure in its many forms and degrees.

Sometimes feelings are very intense and frighten some because we have been taught that the person experiencing intense emotions is out of control and may hurt someone. But individuals who have intense emotions are not dysfunctional and do not necessarily need psychotherapy. Emotions are not disorders; they are simply messages.

Moreover, if a person who was "out of control" was taught that they were just experiencing information from themselves, that it didn't mean that they had to express or act out, then they would not appear out of control, and we would not fear them.

Our teachings are the culprit. We're fine, and with understanding we can be great.

Access to Your Experience and Knowledge

Our serial one-thought-at-a-time thinking brain can perform wonderful feats of logic, reasoning and some recollection. But our experience and knowledge is too vast to be accessed by our serial thinking brain in relevant time frames. Nature's gift comes to the rescue, and just in time. Our emotive system can access our experience and knowledge through feelings.

Our information stores are considerable. Everything we see, hear, sense, taste, and smell and more are recorded and stored, all of this without our conscious effort or mental focus. Emotions are a built-in high speed search and personal information access system, our very own very fast memory access to all of our present and past experiences and knowledge. It should not be surprising that certain feelings are predictive; they help us to foresee and hence plan ahead. When our friends see the emotions on our face, they know how to help us. This ability comes from all of our memory information stores. The challenge is access to our information stores. From a standpoint of recollection in using feelings, we may not remember specifically what somebody said to us, but we remember how they made us feel, and that feeling message would be sufficient. Moreover, the more intense the feeling during storage, the quicker and easier to access later.

21

Feelings give us automatic fast retrieval of memories and sensory data that we need in real-time to make timely decisions. Feelings are the compaction or concentration of many words, specifics, memories and ideas meshed together so that we can get the gist from our vast collection of relevant stored experience and knowledge. This is all accomplished by our wild elephant, emotional makeup, and sent to our conscious mind through a short simple artifact called a feeling.

At times we access our feeling simply by cognitively dwelling on a matter and registering an emotion that is so intense, it cannot be ignored, or so subtle we can barely make it out through very thoughtful introspection. Think about a matter, and we get a feeling. Not always, as not all matters that we think about will trigger an issue we need to address in the moment. The intensity of the feeling carries that information's priority or urgency, so that we can respond appropriately.

Emotions are the substance of sensations, the material of memories, the signals that tell us about what we know from the past and what we are presently experiencing – all from that wealth of information within us.

Guests Bearing Gifts

If somebody were to say to us, "Hey I have a gift for you" and then they gave us a dirty sock, we may laugh or worse, throw it back. Because somebody says it's a gift doesn't make it so. We all can immediately recognize a gift as something we need, something we can use, something that benefits us or something that makes us feel something pleasurable, something we received for free without strings attached. That's a true gift. A guest is quite often a gift we give ourselves. Indeed, our feelings are gifts bearing gifts.

Feelings are gifts, nature's gifts. Often we don't recognize this because we have been taught that some feelings are wrong, some are bad, detrimental, negative, distracting, something we can do without, a hindrance not a help. Some are painful and some are dirty socks to throw back.

Feelings are a wonder of nature. Nature's beauty is more than all around us, it is within us as well. It moves, it flows and it is dynamic. We don't understand the biochemical or neurological mechanics, but fortunately we don't need to for practical use of feelings.

We may accept feelings of joy, excitement, and inspiration as gifts because we have been taught that pleasure is good, but nature does not discriminate. If it did, we would get less than half the information we need to make decisions and to take action. We may not survive or thrive.

All feelings are something we always need, something we can use, and something that is beneficial. Feelings are never wrong with respect to ourselves, and in that way they are a personal truth. Our first step is to accept them all, learn what they mean, and then we will know the truth we are telling ourselves when we are having a feeling.

Superposition of Feelings Rule

A very dear friend, Galina, was telling me that she can hardly stand it when her Aaron is *worried, tired, frustrated.* All that she wants is for him to be *happy.* I relayed my observation to Galina that Aaron is as *happy* as he allows himself to be. What could be better? When he is *worried,* he is telling himself and her that he needs to prepare for something. Ask him what that is and help him prepare. When Aaron is *frustrated,* he is telling himself and her that he has a time problem. Use logistics to figure out a solution or find some more time. When Aaron is *tired,* he is telling himself and her that he needs rest. Find him a place to rest. He will do the same for her. We can address each feeling independently, but our solution can include them all. Your party depends on when your guests arrive and resolution determines when they leave. Gratefully address them all.

Learning the Language for What Purpose?

We learn in stages and build upon learning. We can accept only a quantum of information and only at specific times. We surround ourselves with environment subject to circumstances and situations. We chose a goal or purpose in life if we are fortunate and have certain opportunities. But is that enough? Thoreau wrote:

> "It is not enough to be industrious; so are the ants. What are you industrious about?"

Our life's quest or purpose may change. That would be a sign that there is still some life in us. A sign that we don't just appear and act alive by going through the motions. Thoreau observed:

"The masses of men lead lives of quiet *desperation.*"

Perhaps where we are now headed is not where we want to end up in our life's journey, but we may believe that we have few options left. If so, we would be thinking too much. Desperation is a feeling, one we may be ignoring. As George Eliot wrote:

"It is never too late to be what you might have been."

If oue journey is to be truly challenging, we must be prepared to step into the danger, experience the possibilities, and risk the path less traveled. That is how we progress, find meaning, and develop purpose. At some point in the journey, we will experience danger. The question is, what will we stuff into our backpack to take with us to help meet the challenges?

Feelings are Directional

We are the sole owners and our own authority when it comes to our feelings, but we do not initiate them, they initiate us. One of the most inspirational and motivating speakers today, Anthony Robbins, teaches that we should "plant emotions like seeds in our garden ever day." While I am inspired and moved by this idea, it is counter to my understanding of emotions. In my understanding our feelings are our guidance system in every day behavior and on our life's journey. We receive from emotions and our behavior follows. This does not mean that we cannot choose to do charitable acts or engage in acts of love. Only that when we choose, we act from thoughts, not feelings. We must strive to understand our feelings, not control them. We can't think and practice to feel like professional actors without manipulating ourselves. Acting is a profession unto itself because of this unique requirement. The rest of us must rely on our feelings.

Understanding our emotions does not promise the elimination of heartache, pain, and suffering. However it does mean that we don't experience needless heartache, needless pain, and needless suffering. When we don't address the painful feelings, we stand to encounter more pain, suffering and regret. We know from deep inside us when we could have avoided life's potholes and wrong turns had we read the sign and responded to the signals.

Moreover, we need the signals from the painful feelings to grab our conscious attention, to keep us aware and focused on the cogent issues, so that we are able to make good decisions in real-time. We need pleasurable feelings for positive reinforcement and encouragement. This is the feedback mechanism that tells us that we did something right and we should be rewarded.

At the risk of being repetitive but because it is of vital importance, painful emotions are just as positive and necessary as pleasurable ones. They cumulatively and collectively provide a full set of signals from which we can make better decisions. We are pain reducing, pleasure seeking, survive and thrive beings. We have an internal carrot and stick mechanism built-in to propel and guide us.

Our emotions are a beautifully designed engine to help us survive and thrive, an intelligence hybrid with our cognitive and emotive functions. The efficiency of the thinking-feeling hybrid that we are trumps the thinking engine that we use every day. We are our own authority, because we think and feel, therefore we are.

2 - Difficult to Welcome All the Guests

We override our emotions, control them, circumvent them, minimize them, subvert them, channel them into "positive" feelings, "fuzzify" or ignore them at our peril. When we turn away a feeling, we are discarding vital information, the core issue facing us, the guest at the Guest House door gently knocking.

The irony is that cognitive misunderstanding or ignorance makes us our own worst enemy. The non-use or misuse of feelings, by not addressing the issue at hand, is the method we use to sabotage ourselves. For many, this happens daily. We may get a message from our wild elephant that we don't understand, so we kick our behavior elephant to do something and the behavior elephant acts out. For example, we feel some anger and lash out at the nearest object, without due thought about what we are truly angry about.

We may get another message from our wild elephant that we don't understand and we kick our thinking elephant to make a left turn, as it was trained to do. But our wild elephant told us the left turn is dangerous, the road is too long, that it will end in a dead end, that it is a waste of time, or just plain the wrong way. For example, we get frustrated and change to another task to relieve the frustration. We are headed down the wrong path, that's not what

29

our wild elephant recommended. This won't be the last time we ignore our better senses unless we learn some Elephant.

Simple Enough for a Child and Yet a Mystery

Children naturally use their emotions to learn and to make decisions with little or no knowledge, before language, and experience. It's no wonder that our first signs of intelligence are feelings intelligence. Children have little choice because they lack experience, and yet they advance naturally and quickly by use of emotions through a simple pleasure-pain stimulus-response algorithm that promotes survival.

The bad news is that as we grow, we are mostly taught that feelings are wrong, or that emotions are like our appendix not useful, and even a grave liability when infected.

Highly judgmental and confused teachings are pounded into us. These teachings block any beneficial cognitive and behavioral use of feelings. In our culture, boys are taught that feelings are weak, "girly" and not to be tolerated. We are taught showing fear is weakness, an emotion we should never have if we are indeed a man.

Women are taught that feelings are allowed and sometimes necessary because as women, they are expected to be emotional, weak. Women show this weakness by expressing emotions because supposedly this is a showing of lack self-control. Moreover, girls are taught that anger is ugly and should be avoided.

In addition and to our detriment, our culture teaches us to ignore our painful feelings. As we were growing up we may have heard, "That doesn't hurt, does it?" We are taught to run for drugs at the first feelings of pain. We are taught to avoid things that could cause pain, and if feelings do result, we are scolded and reminded that we should have listened. These cultural teachings are self-reinforcing, and therefore difficult to unlearn. We all learn that pain is bad and to avoid it at all costs. We are taught painful feelings have only one message and that is to find a way to feel good, treat the symptom.

The Bad, the Worse and the Ugly About Theories

Many confused, misguided, and mistaken teachings dominate our psychology and self help field. Some theories and teachings promote the idea that if we don't express our feelings they become bottled up inside and that's not healthy. They admonish us to "free" our feelings, let our feelings out, like so much gas out of a balloon. Some teach that we cannot control what happens in our life, but we can be the master and always control how we feel if you use a little guidance and a few techniques.

Some teach that intense feelings are distortions that cause misbehavior. They need to be channeled to good feelings.

Some teach that anger, jealousy, fear, unhappiness, and other "negative" emotions are the cause of dysfunction. Its simple cause and effect theories teach to eliminate the feelings and we will undoubtedly eliminate the dysfunction. Some

31

theories hold that it's those misguided, distorted or out-of-control emotions that are the real culprits at the root cause of disorders and chaos. So if we can control the feelings, we would have peace and order.

Even the most enlightened teach that bad or "negative" feelings like anger, hate, fear, anxiety, are a fact of life, but need to be minimized or transformed into good, warm, fuzzy feelings.

Mostly, emotive theories teach that feelings are the bad boys that require psychotherapy, self-regulation, coping, adaptation, medication, prayer, and the giving up of inalienable rights to some higher power or worse, authority figure.

The Food, Alcohol, Tobacco, and Drug Barons

To further complicate and obscure matters on emotions, the food, alcohol, tobacco, and pharmaceutical industries have found the chemical means to induce almost any emotion that we wish to have: satiation, appetite, gayety, happiness, immunity to physical pain, sexual arousal, ecstasy, peace, comfort and rest, to name a few. Our culture teaches us to reach for these as soon as pain is encountered or we when we demand pleasure or escape from feelings.

These methods are to be avoided. At least when feelings are chemically induced, our natural emotive guidance system will not function as designed, as we have now artificially chemically induced a feeling, and that will mask natural feeling signals from arising when we need them. Thus we lock the door to more guests coming, to party alone, and without protection for the moment.

I Can't Control the Wild Elephant, She Said

A behavioral psychologist turned activist informed me of her struggle to expose a particular group that was corrupt and abusive. Her efforts thus far had made her frustrated, but she was energized and animated when talking about the matter with me. When she realized that she was visibly angry, she made an apologetic remark, "But it's righteous anger." I asked, "Is there another kind?" So even one behavioral psychologist can benefit by learning Elephant.

As we will see, anger informs us that something is unjust. Actively doing something about the injustice is the very definition of righteous. What we will do about the injustice and how we will go about it will require thinking, decisions, and perhaps action. But the feeling of anger is the first step in the process that puts our gift token at GO.

Just like a gift treasure map, the anger feeling's gift is two-fold. First, the adventure of thinking and moving through the search and second, the treasure at the end is justice or fairness achieved.

Ross, a very close friend, is meticulous and detailed in every aspect of his life. He is very creative, but proud of the fact that he uses logic and reason to make important decisions. We disagree on how much his good decisions are based on logic and how much depended on feelings from just the wealth of knowledge and life experience he embodies in his decisions. The former Chief Justice of the Supreme Court, Charles Evans Hughes would disagree with Ross. He explained how the most important decisions a person can make are made:

> "At the constitutional level where we work, ninety percent of any decision is emotional. The rational part of us supplies the reason for supporting our predilections."

Language Variability

The language of emotions comprises many specific emotions with many different names, synonyms, some of which are similar in meaning but may differ in emotive intensity. Moreover some emotions have various definitions, some of behavioral expressions. A quick check on the word *happy* in a Thesaurus gives:

> blessed, blest, blissful, blithe, can't complain, captivated, cheerful, chipper, chirpy, content, contented, convivial, delighted, ecstatic, elated, exultant, flying high, gay, glad, gleeful, gratified, intoxicated, jolly, joyful, joyous, jubilant, laughing, light, lively, looking good, merry, mirthful, on cloud nine, overjoyed, peaceful, peppy, perky, playful, pleasant, pleased, sparkling, sunny, thrilled, tickled, tickled pink, up, upbeat, walking on air ...

Please note again that some definitions of specific emotions are behaviors closely associated with or descriptive of the emotion, and some are colloquialisms or slang. To reduce duplication, we attempt to provide a unique but not necessarily complete set of emotions. Although there is some variability allowed where the intensity between words describing similar feelings differ enough to warrant distinction, as for example between *happy* and *joyous*.

What is certain to lead us astray is to accept the premise that we can group uniquely different message emotions into groups and deal with them as a member of a group. We have different emotions for a reason, and if the teaching proposes that we can just shove fear in with anger and/or depression, that teaching will not reach the level of the message required for understanding, and the language is then distorted as to become useless.

To better understand our predilections, let's look at specific emotions and their meaning or message, and more deeply learn the language.

3 - A Crowd of Sorrows, the Painful Feelings

In teaching about feelings, the 13th-century Persian poet Rumi wrote in his poem, *Guest House,*

"Welcome and entertain all! Even if they're a crowd of sorrows, who violently sweep your house empty of its furniture, still, treat each guest honorably. He may be clearing you out for some new delight."

Feelings, the guests bearing gifts, bring both simple and complex messages to our conscious thinking mind.

If we can understand that these guests coming to visit our conscious thoughts - "a joy, a depression, a meanness, sorrows..." are ephemeral feelings and each is important enough that we should meet them at the door laughing and invite them in.

To some it will seem common sense, and that is because some have already been inviting in and listening to their guests. Some of us have already learned some Elephant, and it is obvious. Some of the messages from our guests were not so obvious, but we managed. But some didn't speak the language, acted nonchalantly, and quietly closed the door on the guest. What are those messages and what do they mean?

Let's take a closer look at the crowd of sorrows, the painful feelings, their messages and the intelligence they provide.

Anger

Anger is considered one of the most dangerous of emotions, because along with hate, anger is the least understood and most abused message we send ourselves and display to others. Some of us seem to have more anger than others, and there is a simple reason. We all have different temperaments, life experiences, and knowledge. Some of us have suffered abuse of one kind or another. These experiences leave memories of unfairness and injustice, where somebody was not held accountable. When we witness unfairness or injustice, we inherently know that it is a threat to us, and that message is packaged in anger. Martin Luther King said it so eloquently,

> "Injustice anywhere is a threat to justice everywhere."

It is not uncommon to become angry when a police officer issues us a traffic violation. But are we angry with the officer for writing the citation or are we angry at the unfairness of a law forcing us to drive slower than we think safe? Or are we angry because we have heard that the law enforcement is stricter and more expensive because the county needs the revenue and issuing tickets as an unfair additional tax burden? Or are we angry because we are adult and fully capable of ascertaining what is safe? Or are we angry because it's unfair that we live

38

in a democracy, but that our vote has no say in setting speed limits, especially slow ones we think are too low? Our thinking should test each scenario. Ask yourself which it is and you will feel the anger residing on one of more, but perhaps not all of the above issues.

To our detriment, when we get angry, we have been taught that the object of our anger deserves punishment, retribution, payback, and even some hate. The problem is discovering who or what is the true object of the angry feeling.

Misdirected anger is a very common abuse of this emotive signal, giving anger the reputation of an avenger, the instigator or cause of violent behavior. In addition, the fear signal may arise when we see anger, because we inherently understand that the consequences of misdirected anger can create an incendiary and potentially dangerous situation for us.

It seems today, more of us are angry, or at least more than was manifest in the recent past. For most of us, the standard of living was higher and our quality of life was better. Things have changed and not always for the better. We are working harder and earning less. We try to look elsewhere, but there is no hiding from inside us that we are more angry than usual. We see more road rage. The roads are more crowded; it takes longer to get to work and back. We spend less time with out families. Life is unfair and so we are angry. The world is unfair and justice appears elusive. The rich can afford it, but the rest of us can't. Some reach a breaking point where catastrophic behavior follows.

39

In many cases, the anger signal is ignored and therefore compounds. The unfairness or injustice is not resolved by the resulting behavior; it just creates more unfairness. Feelings of anger will not dissipate if the unfairness continues to exist and grows more threatening until somebody "goes postal."

The message of anger is simply that whatever confronts us is unfair or unjust. That is how we recognize injustice when we see it. Try to define justice, it is nearly impossible. But identifying injustice is innate; we instantly get the angrer signal when we see it. There is nothing bad, negative or wrong with the identification of unfairness or injustice. Thus anger is a very positive feeling.

For anger to be useful, the unfairness or injustice must first be identified. Without first understanding and evaluating an issue, a rush to judgment can ensue. The nearest object is assigned the blame. Not finding the true cause of the unfairness, and speeding ahead full throttle is a common misbehavior resulting from misunderstanding anger.

Again, there is nothing wrong, nothing bad, nothing negative with the emotion, signal or message of anger, even intense as it can be. It is our identification of the object of unfairness or injustice that we need to address in our thinking, decision, action, response or remedy, to resolve that feeling of anger. If that message of anger is ignored or misdirected, it will remain as long as the injustice remains.

Anxiety

Anxiety at low intensities is sometimes called nervousness or worry and at high intensities can be quite debilitating. We will only discuss the non-medical emergency feeling of anxiety, those that we should not be addressing with pharmaceutical remedies, hospitalization, or institutionalization.

The Scriptures seem to encourage that we address anxious feelings today, and not tomorrow:

"Take no anxious thought for tomorrow, sufficient for the day is the evil thereof."

Anxiety is the signal from ourselves that something is going to happen, that we may not be sufficiently prepared to manage well in our current state or situation. Therefore, if we did not do our homework, the research, the work that we know we could or should have done, we will feel that figurative tap on our shoulders or that ache in our stomach, reminding us that we still have time that we can still do something to prepare for that impending event.

Very structured people seem to use anxiety well. Because otherwise, they are pulled in too many directions and out of their protective daily structure. They capitulate early, and just do the preparation work necessary to resolve and hence relieve the anxiety. Thus the anxiety feeling works for them, they are generally better prepared, and their performance is enhanced.

For the rest of us, it's generally a feeling that is ignored and we keep the "anxious care for tomorrow" because we don't understand the message of anxiety, to take some care today.

My artist friend, Will, once told me that he has to "time slice" work because he has many projects, and each one has somebody at the end of it. Telling him he had better finish when he promised. Never mind that good art is difficult to impossible to schedule.

Will becomes anxious. He works like a crazy person to finish each project on time. I know because I have been at the end of one of those projects more than once. I asked him if he would finish each project that he committed to do if he didn't feel the anxiety. He thought about this for a minute, Will is nothing if not thoughtful, and said, "Probably not." Will lets his anxiety drive him to deliver on his commitments. He doesn't use an electronic scheduler, fancy newfangled mobile device or watch dog timer on his watch. He cannot afford a personal trainer or secretary. He simply uses his feelings intelligently. Will is superhuman in that respect, because he taps into his power of anxiety, that signal from within that nudges him and says, "It won't paint itself, get to it, and nobody else can do it but you, Will."

The intensity of the anxiety will tell us relative to ourselves, our safety and the security of the people we care about, the urgency or the overall importance of the matter that is making us anxious. Taking some action to prevent harm is necessary, because not being prepared for a potentially damaging eventuality when we know that we should be, leads to trouble. Being prepared in a dynamic environment starts with listening to our anxiety. We all have different levels of coping with impending events and schedules. Anxiety is how we know to prepare for what is up ahead. This kind of feelings intelligence is free and priceless when used. Solutions come with thinking but we first need to know what to think about. So enter *anxiety* to inform us.

We all have a calendar of events that we track consciously or unconsciously. Some think of this power as a premonition, a foretelling. We have a complex mind that searches for patterns and meaning beyond our conscious understanding. Our feeling-thinking brain has remarkable predictive features, and these are in full play every waking and maybe some sleeping moments as well.

Our anxious feeling alerts us to prepare now for something that may happen later, to act now to prevent something adverse from happening later. Our anxiety will likely continue until we have done all we are telling ourselves we can do to prepare. If we believe that we have finished preparing but anxiety remains at the same intensity, we are telling ourselves that there is something that we haven't done yet. Search for more ways to prepare, starting with what we are anxious about, or consult someone who will help you figure out what you haven't done yet. When our readiness is complete, then our anxiety will discharge, as the issue no longer exists.

Apathy

Apathy is the absence of emotion. We are spiritless, having little or no interest or concern, indifferent. Some definitions hold that the suppression of emotion brings about apathy. The behavioral symptoms of apathy are insensibility, sluggishness, and/or indecision. These are red flags of emotive dysfunction and precursors to poor behavior or worse.

Most well designed mechanisms have system failure indicators to tell us when something is not working properly. Our emotional system contains such a feature, apathy.

Because it is healthy and normal to have emotions, the absence of emotions, apathy, is an indication that perhaps a damaging trauma has occurred or one is not well mentally. Studies show that apathy is experienced after witnessing or experiencing horrific acts, such as extreme poverty, violence, catastrophic events, even prolonged verbal abuse.

By the same token, apathy is also known to be associated with various maladies such as: addiction to drugs or alcohol, Alzheimer's disease, Chaga' disease, Creutzfeldt-Jakob disease, dementia, depression, Korsakoff's Syndrome, excessive vitamin D, general fatigue, Huntington's disease, Pick's disease, PSP, schizophrenia, Bipolar Disorder, and others. If a general apathy persists, our best move is to see a doctor, because we are telling ourselves, something is wrong with our emotional guidance system.

Many of us are apathetic about world events, politics and more remote matters. This is not the apathy to which we refer. Having little or no feeling for remote or inconsequential events to us is actually a signal that we have more important matters to confront first, and it is intelligent to act more locally when we are telling ourselves just that. When situations change, so do our feelings.

Boredom

Boredom has a bad name because it means that we are inactive, momentarily with nothing to do, nowhere to be, or without a reason to live. For many, boredom is that dreadful, painful feeling we would give just about anything to avoid. Boredom is therefore a feeling to blame, to escape, or to die from. How many times have you heard, "I'm eating because I'm bored," or "He's a real bore. I couldn't wait to get away."

When kids complain that they're bored, many parents think they are responsible for providing a distraction of some kind, a fun outing to a fast food restaurant, a video, a game, or a movie. Parents who may not have spent sufficient time with their child may feel guilty, feel they owe the child for not being there, and quickly comply with whatever the child requests.

In this case, the parents are confused with their own feeling, the message of guilt, not the child's feeling, the message of boredom. In this way, the true guest is turned away and his message is not addressed. Children learn that when they are bored, the solution is to eat, watch TV, play video games, get a video, or go shopping. Small wonder that overweight, sedentary children are a national health problem and oblivious to their futures.

We have an innate need to accomplish and experiences. However misused, misguided, misunderstood, maligned and blamed, the boredom signal is invaluable because it tells us when we have available time and need to do something else. That is the simple straight message from boredom. We have time, and we are stuck in a time rut. The world doesn't wait, and it's time to move on.

What a positive message! We always know when we're finished, and we need to find something else to do or think about. Deep down we know that even while we sit perfectly still, we are moving through time at the speed of light. A person will need to try many things in life to learn and grow, become secure, independent and to contribute. Our boredom signal is telling us that our time resource is valuable and not to be wasted.

Boredom is an automatic recess bell, a timeout, and the trigger reminding us to segue to another activity or line of thought.

Sometimes we may become bored while talking or listening to somebody. We need to politely extricate ourselves, if we are to apply our feelings intelligence. We are telling ourselves that it is not only beneficial for us; it is beneficial to the speaker. The speaker is wasting their breath on us, and we need to relieve them of that waste, move on to another topic, stop beating a dead horse, or find another person to converse with. Life is short. We will always have miles to go, and from inside, we know when it's time to move along, when we feel bored.

Depression

Depression is telling us that something is wrong, and it is critical to attend to it. At times depression is so debilitating; that we have no desire to do anything. Our life can be effectively stopped by this emotion, and by design. Depression must be that way to grab and hold our full attention. Something vital has desperately gone awry; we're headed into an abyss, a life's dead end. We need to figure out what that is before it becomes fatal. Perhaps we chose the wrong destination, and we need to make a drastic course correction. Perhaps an important relationship is drifting away. Perhaps our life is not going where we truly want it to go and we can't be what we wish to become.

Abraham Lincoln suffered from "severe melancholy," as they called depression in his time. Transportation was poor and Lincoln was forced to walk everywhere. Biographers say he walked constantly. As we know today, physical activity releases endorphins, which are a natural remedy to depression. On these walks, when Lincoln was temporarily relieved from the intense pain of depression, he would formulate and practice his speeches.

We all marvel at some of the simple words Lincoln put together in the way that he did. Many are so remarkable and wise that we have memorialized his words in stone around the United States. I would theorize that Lincoln realized and seized depression's message, which stirred him to walk, ponder, and make notable leaps in understanding and action, far above anything logic and pure thinking could accomplish. He reached down into that debilitating ache of a black hole, and pulled out solutions to individual legal disputes, community issues, and eventually national problems. The decisions he made changed the face of a young nation that would lead the world. Many memorize his *Gettysburg Address* where his simple words of dedication burn into our memories:

> "... that we here highly resolve that these dead shall not have died in vain -- that this nation, under God, shall have a new birth of freedom -- and that government of the people, by the people, for the people, shall not perish from the earth."

Depression produces a discrete change and can be very abrupt. That is because sometimes we need an abrupt shock to get our full attention. Depression is that emotive two-by-four upside the head to help us change direction, and yes it hurts. But in retrospect, sometimes you just have to say, "Thanks, I needed that."

Discomfort

Discomfort is an unpleasant sensation and is also low intensity relative to other painful feelings. For this reason together with our early training and cultural teachings, physical discomfort is generally ignored or not addressed until late. Some teach that overcoming or ignoring discomfort builds character.

However, most of us know we should pay attention to our body when it gives the message of discomfort. The signal of physical discomfort can seem like nothing, yet lead to everything. The message of discomfort informs us that there is something temporarily awry. If we continue to ignore it, the pain compounds and a bigger problem will emerge. Discomfort tells us that something changed or is changing slowly in a detrimental way. And again, we need to attend to the cause.

By ignoring or overriding the signal of discomfort, we could be making a big mistake because a little conscious awareness and attentiveness may save us grievous harm. Because we regularly receive the signal of physical discomfort, we need not ever suffer the slow-boiling frog syndrome. That is change occurs slowly enough, that we ignore the cause, and the effect grows incrementally unchecked until the frog is cooked. Our fate is fixed, and it is too late for remedial action. We are no longer the master of our fate.

In some less than optimal solutions, the physical discomfort appears to ask us to give something up, and we are unwilling. The classic anecdote is the one where the patient tells his doctor that it hurts to bend his knee, and the doctor advises the patient not do that. But that knee didn't decide to hurt by itself; something caused that change. We are telling ourselves to find the cause and fix it. This is where expert advice is helpful.

Rita, is a very competent woman, an educated well informed teacher, avid reader and author with an uncommon amount of common sense. As we were talking about writing, she related that she gave up reading, or drastically reduced her reading. She said it was not as much fun anymore and that she found other things to do. But it still bothered her that she, who all of her life so enjoyed reading, now found herself not indulging a life long passion. She once recounted how much pleasure she derived from reading to her son when he was very young. Despite all of that, she stopped reading for a period of two years before she discovered that she was squinting at the printed word and there was some physical discomfort in reading, where there was none prior. After having her eyes checked and wearing new eyeglasses, Rita regained her passion for reading and continues unimpeded by the change in her physical condition.

Change is inevitable. Nobody stays young and our body's age. We have many parts in our bodies, and they are all critical in one way or another. Feelings of physical discomfort nudge us to recognize when something has changed slightly. We cannot leave our physical parts unattended. Discomfort informs us that we need to take action. Giving up our body's intended and designed use is a very drastic solution with unintended consequences. But deep down we know that others have suffered changes too, and perhaps found a remedy.

Physical discomfort can also be a message that something touching our body is causing some harm, even though it has a legitimate intended purpose and design. Shoes too large or small, an irritating bracelet or ring, synthetic fabric, neck crick from pillow, back pain from sitting in an uncomfortable chair or not sleeping well on a particular stiffness mattress. These are all objects that we use routinely, and we know when perhaps they aren't right for us. Checking for all of these red flags may seem excessive at times, but they can save us time and suffering down the road. The message of discomfort registers in our thoughts for a good reason. It may come as just a light tap on the door. Some guests are shy about coming to the party.

Disrespect

We may feel disrespected by actions or inactions from others who lack regard, esteem, or consideration for us. Although feeling disrespected may not make our day, it does inform us that our position or status in a particular group is changing or is not as stable or recognized as we believed it to be. Knowing our status or position in a group or relationship, informs us of our role in that group or relationship.

We all belong to various groups -- family, work place, club, team, church, temple, community, neighborhood, ethnic group, town, or country. Although our status depends and varies on our membership in a group, each group is unique. Our status differs depending on our position and role in a particular group.

Irv, a company manager is the man in charge of many employees. When Irv tells an employee to do something, he expects that it will be done promptly and without question. Irv's group at work changes hourly and so do status and roles, as each group Irv deals with is unique. Challenges from members in a group or organization when not addressed, will be followed by actions. The disrespect feeling is a precursor, warning us that, a status change has occurred. Perhaps we have changed groups, or there is a hierarchy change in a particular group and our status is being changed. Irv will have completely different relationships at home. Feelings of disrespect at home will mean a changing relationship with a member of the family perhaps.

The animal kingdom is replete with many pecking orders, hierarchies from the alpha position down to the lowest member of the group. Each member has a status in the group, and status is a characteristic in any group hierarchy or social structure. The function of the structure is to distribute the load so that an outside force impinging on any member of the group is spread across the group structure. The social structure must remain flexible but strong. We behave in many unconscious ways to maintain our position in a hierarchy, which provides order, safety, and belonging among other benefits provided.

Feelings of being disrespected can be cautionary notes that a status change or higher authority is present, or signaling a demotion in status in an organization from above our level. The feeling of disrespect can also inform us of undercurrents working to change our status in a particular social relationship or structure. We may need to anticipate or address that shift in position.

Disrespect arises from subtle and not so subtle behaviors. For example insufficiently deferential use of your name, disdainful looks, commands, posture or gestures. In a relationship that has changed by mutual agreement, feelings of disrespect are less likely to occur as we are aware consciously of the change, no need for a signal.

Many are familiar with Homer's *Iliad* and the precipitating event for the war between the Greeks and Trojans. Paris, a prince of Troy, falls in love with Helen, the wife of Menelaus, a King of Sparta. Paris brings Helen back to Troy to be his bride. King Menelaus knows that the message of feeling disrespect is that he will lose status and power in his kingdom and throughout Greece.

The disrespect brings two status shifts – a personal one for the king from his wife and her new partner, and a political one from a competing economic and political power, Troy. The double shift adds to the intensity of the felt disrespect, because the Kings status and the kingdom's status are threatened. The feeling of disrespect will not be resolved until such time as retribution is exacted by the threat's removal. To be accurate, it was not the beautiful face of Helen of Troy that launched a thousand ships, but the disrespect felt by Menelaus launched a thousand ships. Kings are very wary of being disrespected, because they have so much to lose.

Feelings of being disrespected are generally proportional in intensity to the status of the individual in the group. The alpha has much more to loose in a status shift, and so the emotion is of higher intensity and behavior more dramatic. The lowest status member has nothing to loose in a status shift, and may not feel disrespected at all.

Doubt

We all have doubts from time to time. On occasion, jurors are required to decide a case beyond a reasonable doubt. There are religious, spiritual, legal, and psychological understandings of doubt. We all know that doubt is that feeling that tells us we are uncertain.   Addressing the feeling of doubt may cost little, a simple question to someone knowledgeable, or cost much and be very time consuming. A search for additional information or request for production of evidence to support one side of an issue or another may not be easy.

Doubt is a feeling we all get that is largely ignored. Unless the decision is of critical importance, we don't take the time to assemble more data, obtain more evidence or prove an issue one way or another. But that is all that doubt brings, the message from us that informs us that from all that we know and have experienced, we have insufficient information to make a good decision. The matter may not be important enough to warrant more effort to decide the issue, which is for our judgment and thinking to decide. But we have been notified by our doubt as to our true knowledge on the matter.

Doubt, a Hollywood movie starring Streep and Hoffman, showed the classic example of this emotion in play. Streep's character has major doubts regarding Hoffman's behavior toward his young parishioners. She lacks evidence that would ease her doubts, yet she is compelled by her beliefs, which she trusts more than her feelings of doubt. Her doubts tell her that Hoffman could be a good priest, or a bad priest, but she decides that he is a bad priest and charts her course along that path.

We are often beset with a situation in which we have insufficient or imperfect information. How we go about resolving the issue requires thought, strategy, and action. Doubt tells us to find out more, devise a test, do a search, and/or ask a friend or associate. The list of possibilities and strategies is limited only by our resourcefulness. Ignoring feelings of doubt increases our risk of a bad decision or ineffective strategy.

Envy

Envy is the message that we value something that somebody else has and we wish to have that something. A part of us automatically recognizes things that has value to us, and by acquiring that something means that our life could be richer and better.

Envy tells us that if we had the quality that we admire in someone else, then we can be more beautiful, smarter, richer, cooler, or whatever our goal is.

If Billy does better in school because he's smarter, envy tells us that we admire intelligence, and we can go about acquiring some or decide on another goal more suited to our innate qualities or skills. We may not be the sharpest knife, but we may be a hammer, more powerful in another way. Envy gives us clues as to who we are and who we can become by realizing whom we want to be like. Envy is an important feeling, and telling somebody you are envious about something they have can be construed as a compliment.

We learn and grow by examples, choosing models, mentors, or heroes we wish to emulate. We want to be more like them and have what they have. Our envy informs us how to get closer to our goals and purpose. Our envy allows us to discover that we have goals that we were not actively pursuing, or a purpose that we didn't consciously know. Envy has alerted us and given us valuable knowledge regarding the skills and attributes that we need to fulfill our purpose.

Fear

Our understanding of fear confuses us because we are in conflict over whether to honestly expose our feelings and appear weak and vulnerable, or be dishonest and hide it from others. If we hide our fear outwardly, then we must ignore or hide it from ourselves too. Thus we believe, think and act as if fear were our enemy. It grips us. We must control it and must hide its very appearance. This actually slows our thinking down, hides or impedes solutions, and hinders our efforts.

My wizened friend, Justin, told me how he survived during World War II. He learned to cope with fear but by not ignoring the fear, which was difficult because of its intensity and his constant exposure to danger. He supplanted fear with a more compelling focus, and he learned to function fairly well. Justin said, "It is how the hunted becomes the hunter. Learning to fight back helps one control fear."

The classic approach is to control the "grip of fear" so we can become "the hunter." This is the macho traditional response that fear is a paralyzing thing, and if we can control it we can turn the tables on whomever or whatever is causing the fear. We blame the object of our fear and in so doing kill the messenger. But our *fear* is not enemy.

Some teach that the more we fear an enterprise or path, the more vital to our growth that we take it. Those are the seekers of challenge, risk takers, the high rollers, and the ones to be admired in our culture. The logical conclusion would be, do what you fear in order to grow. Again, that is not the message of fear. Fear is not the bully to overcome.

From a practical matter, fear is simply a loud message from us that something or someone as yet unseen or unidentified lurks and poses a potential harm. Danger has many forms and faces, seen, unseen, obvious, and covert. In our lives we will be called upon many times to enter the danger. Fear keeps us consciously informed of the possibility or potential of danger.

We experience fear when our health or safety is not threatened. For example the average person feels the fear of public speaking. This is mostly because of what we are taught and how we are conditioned.

The fear of public speaking is paralyzing, detrimental, and just the opposite of what nature intended. Standing up in front of others, our fear is informing us that there is danger in exposing ourselves to others. Listeners are judging our competence, ability to think and articulate. We are exposing our vulnerabilities. The normal reaction is to protect us from that which may impact our future from associates who will belittle or impugn our competence or abilities. That's a wonderful message to have, a tool that tells us when to be careful.

If we were taught that fear was our friend, we could embrace, listen to, and address our fear feeling, not be encumbered by our fear, we could ask, "Wherein lies the danger?" We have a friend inside, that tells us when we should take care, and that's when we feel the fear signal. Our friend inside is just saying, "Take good care."

The fear signal can be rewired, as with video games. When we play, our fear is desensitized because we build memories of positive impacts from fear. Our experience with war simulations leaves us with feelings of excitement, exhilaration and altogether a fun experience. This is not a problem unless we must decide whether or not we should enlist in the military or do something risky. We should have told ourselves "this is not a game, we could die or worse." Instead, our survival instincts are disabled; we have no fear where plenty is natural. In general, rewiring emotions exposes us to irreparable harm, if we are lucky enough to survive and return, our chances for a normal life are most likely reduced.

Some have gone into a recreational use of fear. Base jumpers, hang gliders, bungee jumpers and others I call fear junkies. Fear junkies exploit the biochemistry involved in the fear signal. Intense feelings of fear will release adrenaline. The adrenaline is part of nature's gift in the fear signal because our natural instinct is to turn and run or fight to the death. Both reactions could use the biological advantage provided by the added physiological power of the adrenaline rush.

But if the fear experienced is very intense, we know that as soon as the danger is overcome, the fear signal discharge is felt as exhilaration. The pleasurable feeling from the adrenaline rush is the relief from danger and that is our body's natural "thank you" message for making the right decision. Hence the addiction to high-risk behavior is due to motivation from that rush. This is not to say that the feeling of exhilaration is bad in any sense, only that when it happens naturally it's nature's gift. If the exhilaration message is from self-stimulation it carries just the pleasure and not necessarily the feeling message. Hence there is a difference, between the application and the recreational use of our feeling signals.

How we deal with any emotion's message is vital. Fear is our first line of defense, forewarned is forearmed is the ancient adage. Sometimes we are faced with a choice between the lesser of two fears. We may fear not having enough money to get through college, and we are forced to take a dangerous job that makes us fear for our life. We weigh the risk of doing things that put us in constant danger against getting food on our table or a college education. We automatically make judgments of the lesser of two evils, and we know it through the intensity of the fear signals we receive from the different fears.

Use fear as part of your rescue package. When you feel the fear, ask yourself, "What are the potential threats? What do I need to do to get around, over, under, by, or through this situation?" After all, we have a mission that crosses many streets; fear tells us when the light is red. Look around, identify and evaluate the potential threat, and make your plans. Then, thank your fear and step into the danger fully armed and ready.

Frustration

The more traditional definitions hold that frustration is the result when one is obstructed from achieving a goal, and the more important the goal, the greater the frustration. Thus, one who is frustrated may exhibit aggressive behavior to achieve the goal. Traditionally frustration is just the evil that pokes its ugly head out to make us more frantic in our efforts.

Our frustration is not that ugly monster. On the contrary, frustration is our automatic internal watchdog timer. Frustration tells us that we have a time problem. Change the speed at which you are working or increase the resources that are presently active in pursuit of your goal. If frustration continues or increases, then the increase in speed or resources was not effective. Frustration is the little estimator inside us, projecting a finish line that will not be attained at our present course and speed. Frustration reports on real-time operational parameters, telling us that we are off schedule, or that our process is ineffective or inefficient, all of which we can change with some time management.

Listening to and addressing our frustration means we never have to fail to achieve our goal on time. Frustration is closely linked to our internal clock and performance estimator. There are too many variables to track in our cognitive thinking brain. But we have the internal workings that track all the variables all at once, in parallel, so that we get the message of frustration exactly at the right time and space, as soon as our wild elephant figured it out and told us through the feeling of frustration. How could that possibly be a negative feeling?

Frustration is the father of invention because it provides us with the capability to know that we need to and indeed can become more efficient, easier, better, and faster. Once we have identified a time problem, we can think about how to solve it. The thinking and execution, 99% perspiration, are subsequent steps. Our feeling of frustration, the vital 1% got us started. That is the intelligence we are giving ourselves when we feel frustration. We will continue to have frustration as long as we attempt any task that takes longer than it should or has a deadline, artificial or otherwise.

Greed

Greed is generally associated with an avid desire for gain or wealth, beyond our deserved or rightful share. Greed is therefore labeled a negative emotion, because it is so closely associated with behaviors like theft, fraud, embezzlement, and idolatry. Greed is one of the deadly sins and traditionally carries a very evil face. The Wall Street greed argument justifies the exploitation of people and businesses because it supposedly builds a more competitive market. But we all recognize it as the ends justify the means argument. For this reason, greed is associated with and leads to graft and unfair business practices, living up to its bad name.

But greediness for knowledge, fame, praise, celebrity, and recognition are personal and socially laudable things. Thus, greed itself is not the culprit; it is the characteristic behavior generally following greed which earns it that name and we need to recognize positive aspects of a very good signal.

I read and listen to my friends say the 2008 financial collapse was all due to greedy bankers, greedy brokers, and greedy ratings makers. But is a dog that systematically and habitually buries bones, greedy? That dog doesn't know any better, and that's what a dog does. The dog is motivated the bones are a dog's treasure, yet a dog is not greedy.

That greed is an emotion closely tied to bad behavior is well known. But the emotions we should be worried about necessarily are complacency, arrogance and contempt, and not from bankers, brokers and candlestick makers. The bank collapse was due to Congress' complacency that assisted Wall Street in systematically removing all the legal safeguards that kept the financial system strong.

The collapse came about because in all their arrogance, the Federal Reserve assumed unregulated financial markets were going to regulate themselves equitably. The collapse came because the Bush administration's contempt for the rule of law systematically dismantled all of the people's regulatory watchdogs and created industry lap dogs. The real culprits had power so they weren't greedy, they were just complacent, arrogant, and contemptuous. Greed had a part, no doubt.

But let's not forget that blame is only productive for finding breaking points and then for repairing them. Not addressing the proper triggered emotions only finds partial solutions, and sometimes injustice, as the unaddressed triggered emotions will remain to cause unnecessary pain another day. Generally, an emotion's message is unaddressed, the issues are unresolved, the root causes continue to exist.

Greed's message is motivation. This signal drives squirrels to store up for the winter. Likewise greed is the guest that calls when we need to store up for a predictably bleaker future. Ambition is sometimes seen as a greed for power, which can be for a good or bad purpose. Money is the most obvious thing to store up to secure our future, but skills and other things of value can also be the objects of greed. Greed will drive a person to work harder in the present for a better future.

When we feel greedy, we are painting a better future and informing ourselves that it is possible for us to attain that future. We can study, research, make deals, and/or pursue other activities in the present to achieve a possible future. Greed is the driver. The greed message informs us of our goal, and that we can attain it if we actively work to achieve it.

Guilt

We hear the guilt signal when we realized that did something wrong and now must it make right or make amends. Guilt informs us that we are not perfect or infallible. Mistakes and misjudgments are always possible.

Without guilt, we would have trouble knowing when we did something inappropriate, unjustified, unfair, or overreacted and caused harm. The message of guilt is to make something that you did wrong right.

Deep down in our being, we know that injustice festers and never disappears without some reconciliation. If we had a hand in dispensing that injustice, we may feel guilty to remind us to go back and make amends. Deep down we know that roles may be reversed in the future. A wrong not righted is a wrong not addressed, is a wrong long remembered and a wrong to be avenged.

A group of veterans from WW II for many years felt the guilt of killing Japanese soldiers and civilians, even though it was deemed necessary and sanctioned by our government. The feelings of guilt superseded the peace that was made between the soldiers and countries. But the feelings of guilt would not die. These veterans took it upon themselves to address the guilt. They contacted Japanese veterans and opened a dialog. Then they had meetings to commemorate the battles, to forgive, and to show respect for each other. Although friends were lost, because of guilt, friends were made. By reaching out, understanding grew and enemies became friends, which would otherwise not have happened without the mutual feelings of guilt. What a wonderful result occurred when these soldiers addressed their guilt.

Although painful, the guilt message itself is positive. Guilt helps maintain a peaceful balance between others and ourselves automatically, if we honor it. The guilt signal is part of our personal feedback system; we acted, the action exceeded some personal norm, we receive the guilt signal so that we can rectify our action.

Hate

Hate is the message we receive when we are telling ourselves we need to withdraw, and create distance between the hated object and ourselves. The hate feeling can start with dislike, but in very intense forms, hate is the natural feeling of being repulsed. Nature gave us this so that when we see something in conflict with our knowledge or beliefs, something repugnant, we need to back off and gain some distance.

The hated object may not be a threat, but proximity can make it one, especially if we misinterpret intent or something about the objects response character. When we hate something or someone, hate is telling us that if we seek an interaction without addressing our feelings or changing our understanding, the interaction will turn out badly and reinforce ignorance.

Some believe hate and fear are different sides of the same coin, related. Sometimes fear can lead to hate, but fear indicates that danger lurks. Hate informs us that there is something we see that we don't understand, and we need to withdraw and gain understanding.

Hate is the classic example of ignored messages, especially when the one experiencing the hate manifests unlawful behavior as a result of this feeling. We have been taught that hate means the hated has no right to exist, and sometimes they must be punished or eradicated. Hate has many names; in a social group general low intensity hate manifests as discrimination. An individual's high intensity hate can turn into a hate crime, violence against another for no other reason than a feeling of hate.

Hate is a precursor signal that tells us uncontrolled interaction should be avoided because it may be detrimental to health and safety. Intense hate leads to violence in situations where understanding is severely lacking. Race riots are examples of premature interaction. The law attempts to protect people from violence and sometimes from hate. But the law can only be applied in the aftermath. To be used properly, hate needs to be recognized, examined, and accounted for in our societal planning process. This can be done by decreasing proximity between hating factions, with staged or tiered knowledge sharing, measured sharing situations, and circumstances to familiarize the parties with each other. When understanding arrives, hate leaves.

But there is power in hate's signal, it's natural intended use. Identification of hate and the automatic building of understanding, are the first steps to discovery and therefore resolution, learning, and progress. Without addressing the hate message, discovery and growth would be more random and progress much slower. Therefore from time to time, we will feel hate or even a strong dislike. If our strategy for adventure and discovery is naturally less rigid or our initial interactions are generally favorable experiences, then we won't feel hate as it's not needed.

Have hate or strong dislike? Seek understanding, slowly build relationships, and proceed with caution. If the hate leaves, you've built a solid foundation of understanding. If hate lingers, reduce you distance and study further.

Hate's message tells us to safely reevaluate our beliefs about the hated, because our beliefs are insufficient and imperfect, our information is inadequate, and interaction now would not be mutually beneficial. Without hate, we are that proverbial bull in a China shop. Hate is a vitally necessary message, because we can destroy priceless things without intention with just ignorance. Hate tells us to step back and learn – then step up and engage.

Helpless

The message of helpless is simple – get help. It sounds easy enough, but amazingly difficult to apply because of poor teaching. Noam Chomsky describes the typical application of helplessness in our culture as:

> "All over the place, from the popular culture to the propaganda system, there is constant pressure to make people feel that they are helpless, that the only role they can have is to ratify decisions and to consume."

That is how the intellectual views helplessness. The helpless are those who lack power to exercise basic rights. Our academic teachings do not currently recognize feelings and steadfastly ignore the message of helplessness. If we were taught that when we feel helpless, we are informing ourselves that we need to find help, then we would not look to ratify decisions or consume unless these were remedial to our feelings of helplessness. Moreover, people that can consume or ratify decisions are not truly helpless. They have a power they are not using. This is yet another example of how we work against our best interests when we ignore our feelings.

We are defeated by our thinking, not our feelings. Feelings of helplessness tell us to get help, find allies, organize, and use what advantages and resources we have to resolve our helpless condition or dire situation. In some ways Chompsky accurately represents that pressure in our culture is used to persuade purchases or induce and coerce compliance to power. But ratification means capitulation to the applied pressure by not addressing the message of helplessness. Compliance to pressure does not resolve but instead compounds the feeling of helplessness.

In closed societies, the helpless are allied by their common helplessness, and there is power in numbers. The feeling of helplessness can be a very powerful feeling when addressed and dangerous to tyrants and despots.

Our helplessness message informs us that we have choices and that we are not exercising them. We are an infinitely creative species, and have it within us to cognitively seek out alternatives when it is in our best interest to do so. Helplessness tells us when to do that.

Hopelessness

The hopeless feeling generally comes to us in difficult times, so it is easily ignored or quickly overlooked. During these times many things threaten us consciously and win the competition for our immediate attention. The hopelessness message is often discarded as a distraction because it travels with fear, desperation, and other painful feelings that are more intense and receive our more immediate attention. Never-the-less, all feelings have issues which must be addressed in some order to properly apply our feelings intelligence.

The message of hopeless is simple; find hope! Finding a reason for hope increases our chances of survival and success and is like all the other emotions, an important signal from ourselves to implement our prime directive by addressing a certain pressing issue in some way.

In the siege of Stalingrad, one of the bloodiest conflicts in World War II, the Soviets were fighting a loosing battle against the much better armed and organized German threat. Within hours of the first wave of the blitzkrieg, Stalingrad became an inferno, as 1,000 German planes carpet-bombed an industrial city filled with wooden houses and oil tanks. Hundreds of families were buried alive in the rubble of fallen buildings. The horror had only begun. With bitter cold, dwindling and exhausted resources and starvation, the Russians found themselves desperate and dying. Fighting a seemingly unstoppable and much stronger foe, the Russians felt hopeless.

During their bleakest period of the war and darkest hour, Danilov, a Russian officer, suggested that they find a hero. What is notable is that all Russians felt hopeless and looked for strategies, but few addressed the hopelessness message because of other more intense feelings. Danilov addressed the hopelessness message, that in order to win, they needed to find hope. He provided them with a hero, a sharpshooter, Zaytsev, who was so successful, that his heroics rallied and strengthened the resolve and will of the Russian people of Stalingrad. When all seemed lost, hope was rekindled.

Zaystsev twice won the highest medal that the Russians gave. This tremendous honor bestowed from a superpower in gratitude to a young man, for providing them with hope that was instrumental in prevailing against insurmountable odds at the most desperate of times. What an amazing feeling hopelessness is, and bizarrely ironic because it always comes at the worst possible time but is always timely. That is the power of the feeling of hopelessness, that it can turn the tide in a world war.

Humiliation

A good general knows when to retreat. And we are all that General as we take control in our own life. But how does the General know when to retreat? We will feel humiliated.

Humiliation makes us feel smaller, weaker, and incompetent against a much stronger, more powerful entity. The message of humiliation is to acknowledge the more powerful force that confronts us. Humiliation provides a strategy for survival. That is to expose our throat to the humiliation, because that is our best chance for survival. "Better a live dog than dead lion" is the adage and the strategy. Humiliation tells us that we are not the biggest, smartest, strongest, more powerful being in an encounter. But we must live and even play with those who are. Nature gave us other strengths and skills, we need time to figure out what they are and hone them. The feeling of humiliation gives us that time.

Hunger

Such an obvious but very ignored feeling. Why bring even bring it up? Because we live in the land of plenty, hunger's message is often ignored. The message of hunger is that we need food nourishment because our energy is diminishing.

Where food is abundant the importance of feeling hunger is lost on us because the practice of eating is routine and the hunger signal is preempted. However, without the hunger feeling we would not know that we needed sustenance for our body. That would lead to malnourishment, followed by certain death. The message of hunger is learned early and quickly and the resolution for hunger is to eat until satiation. Satiation is a pleasurable feeling that signals we have sufficient to sustain our body for yet a while longer; we're full now and should stop eating.

Eating is the learned activity that resolves the hunger feeling. But in today's primarily in industrialized nations, the food industry has found ways to disable the feeling of satiation, the signal that we have eaten enough.

Mass food producers have discovered that if we don't know when to stop eating, food sales are higher. And so, we have a paradoxical food problem with 400 million worldwide obese people and even more living in starvation. We see our kids eating processed food, unable to stop them from consuming more calories than they can expend, more than they naturally need.

The pharmaceutical industry solves obesity by chemically blunting the hungry feeling through appetite suppressants. This may work as long as the suppressants are taken, but often with severe side effects. Once off suppressants, the hunger comes back, and usually more intensely than before. This starts a vicious cycle, the yo-yo diet that plagues many who for whatever reason have rewired the satiation feeling.

The lesson to be learned is that tinkering with the natural functioning of any of our feelings is disruptive and potentially lethal. Our navigational system, when gamed, will not perform as designed. Thinking we can game the system, we will quickly find ourselves at war with ourselves. A war we will lose.

Loneliness

Bees have hives, ants have colonies, and wolves live in packs. The animal kingdom teaches us that whether you live in a hive, run with a herd, or hunt in a pack, there is strength in numbers and together we are stronger. The lonely feeling is community glue. We are social creatures and live in societies.

Loneliness is the message that we need to connect with somebody, to establish communication or have an interaction that will provide some kind of bond or social connection.

We inherently know that we live better and we are more likely to survive when we have companionship, camaraderie, and connection. Studies show that the elderly with pets generally live longer and happier. Married people live on the average longer than single people.

Without the lonely feeling, many would be oblivious to relationships outside our basic needs to procreate. Friendship would be tougher to come by, as there would be less need for a friend. Friendship is a great strategy for survival and thrival. The lonely feeling compels us to seek meaningful relationships because we know that a companion makes the journey safer, more possible and more fulfilling. Loneliness provides the need for society, and therefore groups grow and cultures flourish.

Feelings of loneliness can arise regardless of our position of security or power. We may not have read Aesop's Fable, *The Lion and the Mouse*, but we inherently know of the principle, the weakest can help the strongest, depending on the situation and circumstances. When we feel lonely, we inform ourselves to seek companionship and connection with others. Life is complex and circumstances change in unpredictable ways. Without loneliness, our need for others and for friends would be reduced, along with our chances for survival in a vastly unpredictable and complex world.

Pain

Physical Pain. When we receive the physical pain signal we generally turn our attention to where the pain is coming from to identify the paid source and the severity. Intensity can help us with the diagnosis.

For example, if the pain is in the neck, we first think it's muscle related, because that's mostly what is there and the most frequent cause of neck pain. It also could be nerves, sinew, or bone, but we go down the possibility tree looking for the most obvious first, and then branching to the other possibilities in their probable cause priority. Finding complete solutions more efficiently is our feeling's intelligence, because we first identified the feeling, localized that source, registered the intensity of the feeling, and then checked in with our conscious thinking to recall information that we have for that particular kind of pain.

Not finding something, we seek help from an expert - mom first, then our friends, Internet, a doctor, or religious practitioner. That is learned behavior and your mileage will vary with your knowledge and beliefs. Our solution or healing will arrive through the thinking of solutions, and will depend on who or what we trust. But the need for healing will come in the form of pain first.

There is a very important note to be made here about process. First, the pain feeling told us that there was a problem. Second, we needed to focus on an issue, a physical pain at a specific location. Third, we determined the severity of that problem from a survival standpoint, and finally we determined the problem's priority with regard to everything else we were facing at that particular moment. All these were registered in our conscious thinking, which then and only then, started us searching for solutions, options, schedules, more information, communication, and action in general.

But to drive the nail home that sequence of events all started with a feeling, one that we did not ignore and one in which we did not kill the messenger. Without that very positive feeling of pain from an injury we could easily bleed to death and have the ability to stop the bleeding, but not know that we needed to.

Our tolerance to physical pain based on beliefs, teachings and conditioning, makes us vulnerable. It makes such a discrete and profound difference in our personality, presence, and our outlook on life when we are pain free. Relief is so immediate and change so discrete; we naturally learn that if we can eliminate physical pain, we should.

Although some teach that ignoring pain makes us stronger, we intuitively know that the message of physical pain is focus attention and search for its source. Our feelings intelligence tells us our chances are best when we discover the cause of the pain earlier rather than later.

Emotional pain can be triggered from an external object. "What a pain." "He's a real pain in the neck." Similar expressions are used in many languages and cultures. They all mean the same thing, that we felt angst, a disturbance in our comfort; some level of hurt, and that consciously registered the feeling of some emotive pain.

That "royal pain in the neck" is triggered by past pain memories or projections for unfavorable futures. Emotional pain can come from painful feelings like fear, anger, envy, or suspicion. The source may be resonant in the observer for many reasons. When we register emotional pain, we can identify the source, identify the emotion, address the emotion message, and resolve it by creating solutions of when, how, and what to do and then taking the correct action.

Rejection

We all have felt rejection when our advances are not accepted or when we are not "good enough." Rejection is the opposite of the feeling of acceptance. As in any social situation, where we apply for membership to a group or relationship, there are criteria for acceptance. If we fail to pass muster, we will feel rejection.

We can feel rejected by the opposite gender, cliques, peers, groups, associations, and other social structures. In the very young, rejection is more common and more painful. As we mature, we are able to form more complex relationships and rejection is less intense. The message of rejection is simply that you cannot enter into this relationship or group.

The feelings of rejection may be followed by teasing, ridicule, ostracizing, bullying and other adverse behaviors. The feeling of rejection is labeled "negative" and is to be avoided in our culture. Moreover, feeling rejected can lead to other painful feelings like loneliness, aggression, depression, and in general lower confidence and self-esteem.

But what is the powerful information that we can discover when we feel rejected? The rejecting individual or group believes that we are deficient or inferior against a standard or criteria that they espouse. We can discover their criteria or grounds for rejection and perhaps remedy our deficiency if we want to join badly enough, changing ourselves in some beneficial way if that standard or criteria improved our skills or behavior in some fashion.

But more importantly, we also learn about the individual or group that rejected us - what their most important beliefs are and what gives them comfort or security – what is their true interest or motivation. Rejection allows us a second chance to evaluate our desire for the relationship or membership where it clashes with our own beliefs or standards. As Woody Allen put it:

"I'd never join a club that would allow a person like me to become a member."

An added bonus of the message of rejection is that that joining the relationship or group may not be the best thing for us. If we are incompatible in some invisible way, that incompatibility will promote a confrontation and parting in the future. Not joining is then a time saver, and opens the door to other opportunities.

The message of rejection means that we aren't burdened with determining if we should be in a particular relationship or group, since it is decided for us. From rejection we therefore learn to be more efficient at seeking relationships, alliances and group memberships.

Resentment

Resentment tells us that there was an investment of time, energy, or money spent on something or someone, and that something or someone did not reward our efforts as expected. Resentment tells us that we made a mistake or that we have a misconception that we need corrected.

Julie is divorced, but she still resents her ex-husband. Why should she? They are divorced. Julie is informing herself that she invested too much in her ex-husband and should not invest anymore. Her sharing was not reciprocated in the way she expected. Julie may be feeling lonely and she wants companionship. It's natural that she would call her ex, as that may be her ingrained pattern. But the resentment is telling her that would not be wise, because she is not going to get back what she put in and now needs.

We are part of social structures; we have expectations, statuses, pecking order, entitlements and even social duties. When we feel resentment, we are telling ourselves someone didn't live up to his or her assigned duty to us. We were entitled to and expected acts from somebody that didn't materialize.

We are left at a deficit, and our judgment failed. Our resentment message is telling us to reevaluate our agreement, expressed, implied or inferred. Where there is a failure to perform as we expected, possibly after an investment of time, energy or money, we get the feeling of resentment, the message that tells us we made a mistake or have a misconception that we need corrected.

Resentment will tell us not to invest our energy or place reliance there again. When we experience resentment, there may be a tendency to linger and wallow. We are telling ourselves that we may have old patterns to discard. You've been notified by a feeling of resentment, so get moving; you've wasted enough time and energy.

Sadness

Most of us have suffered a loss of a parent, a loved one, a close friend, a sibling, a mentor, a priceless object or even something more abstract like hope. Some of us have gone through a relationship breakup or divorce. These losses bring the feeling of sadness. Some are more distressing and heart rending than others. At high intensities the sadness feeling can come in painful waves. What is that sad feeling telling us and how can it possibly be positive or good? How does it help us survive and thrive to remember that we had friends, people we cared about, something we appreciated dearly, and now they are gone?

The sad feeling is notifying us of loss. Yes, we may have gotten the news somehow or somebody told us, but the conscious notification is not what gives us the sad feeling. The sad feeling is the assessment we make from within ourselves as to the magnitude of our very subjective and personal loss. That is why it's so painful; we need that sad feeling to get our conscious attention. The intensity of the sad feeling tells us quantitatively how much we miss or are going to miss what we lost and how much we depended on them. The intensity of the sad feeling tells us how impactful the loss is to us and why.

Moving forward, the sad feeling reports our loss. This loss has a bearing on our future. We need to reevaluate any reliance we had on the person, place, or thing that is no longer.

It is as if we were a ship's captain, and a gale wind pushed us onto a rocky shoal that punctured our ship's hull. We need to know how big the hole is and where it is with respect to the water line. If the sail was torn or our rudder was broken, we need to know. Our journey depends on many things. We depend on the crew, and our survival depends on our ability to withstand and survive a storm, when we are out to sea. Any loss of propulsion needs to be quantified, accounted for, and repaired or replaced.

This is a physical situation, but deep down we know that our relationships, our friends, our family, our hopes and dreams, provide the support network, that we need along the way. We need to know where a loss will affect our ability to survive and thrive. As we listen to the sad signal, we assess our capabilities and resources to make adjustments for the loss.

Losses are also tremendous learning and growth experiences, as we automatically adjust, grow and adapt to make up the loss. To do this we need to know where to start repairs and sometimes that takes time. Our sadness continues until we have made the patches and repairs. Some losses cannot be recouped. They are irreplaceable and/or irreparable. These losses can render us in a state that cannot be made whole again. However, without that sad feeling, we would continue on a false reliance, not reality. That is the positive message from the sad feeling. Count the loss, and commemorate the love and help we received.

Our losses have a bearing on our future, because depending on the type and extent of the loss, we are less secure, less able, damaged and require recovery. We found comfort and security in a friend, partner or parent, and now they are gone.

But sadness also tells us that there was something worthwhile that happened. That we lived, found comfort, we laughed and that was valuable to our life experience. We thrived in those priceless moments of comfort, joy, security, companionship, and camaraderie. The sad feeling retrieves that memory to our conscious mind in its message. It's good and positive that we remember them and the lessons learned as often as we need.

John, a friend I made in school, confided an observation to me. One evening after study he told me that after his wife lost her father, their relationship became stronger, deeper, and much closer. I never knew the significance of that, or why John told me. But John was very intuitive, and it was odd, which is probably why I remembered. Today I understand, when we suffer a loss, we naturally find ways to replace the loss by making new relationships or strengthening existing ones.

Sometimes, the sad feeling reminds us of someone or something we let go of, a forced loss, perhaps one we can repair because it's unfinished business. Perhaps it was a loss we thought we could sustain, and moved on for other reasons. Without sadness, we would never have a need to go back for something or someone, but sometimes we need to. That's the message of sad, that we lost something of great value, something or someone that we truly needed and relied on. It's necessary and positive that we account for that loss.

Shame

Shame is painful. Many therapies teach us to root out this feeling, to help sufferers, to explain that this feeling hurts us unjustly. We are taught to put away the feelings of shame, attempt not to feel shame, mark it as unfair. Often, shame travels with fear and or anger, which make it more difficult to handle the shame information. Why do we experience shame?

Shame is the feeling we get when we violate or exceed some group or societal norm, responsibility boundary or rule, and it becomes known to the group or authority. The shame feeling originates from the personal behavior evaluator inside each of us, which tells us that we violated the group's rules, and that the consequences of our actions are likely to visit us in a detrimental way.

Shame is nature's way to help us maintain harmony in groups, to warn us when societal rules and norms are not being respected. Without the compliance to norms of behavior, society could not function. Unchecked individual behavior would eventually disrupt and cripple the group. Hence we have shame, a personal evaluator that helps us stay in harmony within our group.

The message of shame warns us of the group remedy for bad social behavior. If we disrespected somebody who has some authority over us, and that becomes known, we feel shame. We are telling ourselves that we have lost trust and status in our group. We are informing ourselves by shame because we may need to take some remedial actions; explain ourselves, gain understanding and support, apologize, and make amends or whatever it takes to win back the group's trust. In most modern cultures, that is all that is required, and is sufficient to address the shame signal.

Sometimes the shame is so intense, we feel that the "bad" act is irreparable. With very intense shame, we are informing ourselves that the cost of remedial action or restitution may be higher than we are willing to pay. In which case, we are well informed because we don't have the capability to pay back or remedy the situation. We need to weigh other options. Some may be drastic, move on with our life in another group or society, move to a new location, find unbiased support, and forgive ourselves.

Sometimes we incur the shame signal through vicarious liability. Somebody in our family or group did something to diminish our status in the group and this becomes known. We are so closely related to the "bad one," we will be judged also. We know that our reputation and status will suffer, or that we will incur retribution from the group. Shame is informing us that we need to take stock in what and whom we can trust. That is the intelligence in shame.

Years ago, one woman with much status in her community, whose teenage daughter got pregnant out of wedlock, withdrew from all community involvement, activities, and her friends. Her shame for her daughter was so great that she did not venture out much for fear of seeing somebody she knew. After all, her daughter got pregnant out of wedlock, which was taboo. This implied that she was a negligent and poor mother.

At first she became estranged from her daughter, but after a short time, she found that she had the time to care for her granddaughter. She accepted her role as grandmother and a close relationship resulted. She provided care for her granddaughter, because the mother was too young and without a husband to help raise the child. The grandmother never regained her small town status, choosing to stay close to her growing family instead. But when her husband died and her children moved on, she moved on with them. Without the shame, her life may have been drastically different.

More recently, we have had a similar event with a U.S. governor and U.S. vice-presidential candidate from a very small town. The governor's unmarried, teenage daughter became pregnant. Although the details received national media attention, the governor exhibited no shame and little embarrassment. Perhaps societal norms have changed, but the governor then acquired trust issues. Many people could not trust that the governor's rhetoric on strong family standards was genuine, because strong family values would have perhaps brought some shame or regret, something she clearly did not have. The only conclusion one could make is that the governor did not really espouse traditional family values or that they were of lesser importance than she claimed. That painted her as hypocritical, two-faced. Politicians are difficult enough to believe, and hypocrisy makes it nearly impossible.

A bankruptcy or foreclosure will bring the shame signal. As borrowers, we feel the shame if we cannot pay back the loan as promised, and request that our debts be forgiven, because we cannot fulfill a societal expectation of contractual payback. The shame message is telling us that lenders are not likely to lend us money in the future because we breached our obligation. This will make our life harder, as they intend that it should. That is the message of shame; some action you took will make your life harder in the future, as your credit is drastically reduced along with your options, decreasing your ability to sustain yourself.

Surprise

Surprise informs us that we did not expect something. The simple message of surprise is to react, because you don't have time to think. The feeling of surprise also informs you that you were not prepared for an event. Surprise does not discriminate. The surprising event may be good fortune or misfortune. An event occurred which was unexpected, without warning and you were taken unawares. Also, surprise is a response intensifier, because if it precedes a pleasurable feeling, the emotional shift is greater, more pleasurable. If the surprise feeling precedes a painful emotion, we experience shock, and we need to react without thinking too much.

We get surprised on occasion to remind us that there is a very large world out there. The message of surprise is a reminder that we need to plan for contingencies, surprises. Without feelings of surprise, we become complacent because our experience fills up with similar data. Our lives become more predictable, more routine, and we stagnate. Your first surprise birthday party rarely has that same intensity again. We automatically build in expectations, making us more prepared for the unexpected event. Life is full of surprises, which makes for a more interesting ride. However, it is difficult to plan for contingencies without the experience of feeling surprised.

On occasion, we like to surprise somebody. This is perhaps because we want to see a true, unedited or unrehearsed reaction from an individual. In some ways this is a test we use to ensure that what we believe about somebody is true. A response without thought filters engaged, comes directly from the heart and sometimes that is what we want.

Tiredness

Studies show that many of us are sleep deprived. Most of us wish at one time or another that we didn't get tired. We hate being tired and admire the tireless. When we get that tired feeling, we just want to turn alert off. That's when we reach for the caffeine. But if we didn't get tired, or we chemically masked the feeling of being tired, like caffeine tends to do, we would not know we needed to find a safe place to rest. If we didn't feel tired, we would not bother with rest, and we would die from exhaustion in short order.

Depriving ourselves of rest chemically will not resolve the tired feeling and will leave us unable to concentrate, falling asleep while actively performing some function, and even hallucination when sleep deprivation is extended. Like many feelings, we can postpone the message of tiredness by chemical means. But we will eventually have to face the reality that our body will need rest and rejuvenation.

The body acts to get the vital rest it needs so that we do not incur an irreparable consequence. Moreover, it is said we are bi-phasic sleepers, which means we're meant to sleep in bouts, not long stretches. If we heed ourselves when the tiredness signal arrives, we will maximize our learning capabilities. New findings indicate that sleep is needed to clear the brain's short-term memory storage and make room for new information

On the incentive side, studies show that people live longer and healthier when their lifestyles incorporate naps during the day, rest periods at peak temperature hours, or regular eight-hour stretches of restful sleep. Individuals who listen to their tiredness feelings and build in longevity by simply addressing the tired feeling and integrating a nap into their daily lives.

Mothers with children understand tiredness, and even look forward to this feeling. They know that a child who has had a certain amount of activity will eventually run out of energy and grow tired. Rest will come automatically as the child will exhaust him or her-self and drops, in compliance with the tired feeling. Then the mother gets a rest too, so she can plan her rest around her child's. That's feeling intelligence all mothers know and practice daily.

We can also be mentally tired. The message of mental tiredness is that we must give that line of thought a rest and move to something else, something different.

If we did not have such a thing as a tiredness signal or chose to ignore it, we would drop from exhaustion within a few days, as the body will shut down, perhaps not so gracefully and when we least desire. That tired feeling saves us from exhaustion. Plan for it.

Unappreciated

To be unappreciated means we don't feel recognized for our effort, quality, or worth. Un-appreciation let's us know that whatever we have done for other(s) is lesser valued than we thought. We are informing ourselves that we overestimated our contribution or that we invested too much for the return.

Reciprocity is a most important ingredient in a relationship. If we don't feel appreciated, perhaps the relationship is deteriorating, or what we put into the relationship was not sufficient. The other is telling us, is that we need to provide something more. Once we know this, from feeling unappreciated, we can consciously decide what and how to improve or save the relationship, or accept that the relationship is not worth changing for ourselves. Either way, you can now make an informed decision, as to where the issue lies, and what you need to do, because you felt unappreciated.

Perhaps you feel unappreciated at our work place. If the unappreciated feeling points at our boss, we may be on the next layoff list, unless we figure out why our work or performance is not sufficiently valued. Our work may be exemplary, but perhaps we personally clash with others. The feeling of un-appreciation is telling us that we need to improve in that area.

Check for other feelings, as there may be other dynamics at play. Feeling unappreciated can indicate that the receiver of your efforts is not as alert as he or she should be, and perhaps not someone you should rely too heavily on. Being unappreciated can also indicate that the other's focus or attention may not be on us.

The value of a contribution is in the eye of the one benefiting. Service or benefits to others will be weighted and valued by those receiving the service, inherently, if not expressly. Feeling unappreciated tells us that our contribution value was not valued as highly as we expected, from the receiver's acknowledgment or lack of sufficient acknowledgment. Compensation is a very important part of advancing in any hierarchy or structure. Unappreciated means no advancement. To resolve that feeling we may need to change our efforts or get feedback as to how or what we can change.

4 - New Delights, Pleasurable Feelings

Pleasurable feelings have always been accepted as rewards and achievements because they are closely associated with good healthy living. Some believe pleasurable feelings are rewards for spiritual living. *"Don't worry be happy," "Achieve Happiness," "Happy is a state of being,"* and many more book titles and admonitions abound. What does it take to make you happy? Pleasurable feelings have a special place in our culture and teachings; they are our most favored guests. Albert Einstein offered it for the feelings of wonder and amazement in this way:

> "The finest thing that we can experience is the mysterious. It is the fundamental emotion which stands at the cradle of true art and true science. He who does not know it and can no longer *wonder*, no longer feel *amazement*, is as good as dead, a snuffed-out candle."

But what are pleasurable feelings really telling us, and what are their messages?

Acceptance

We are social creatures and use the vetting process to control access to many important groups, associations, and institutions in which we are stakeholders. These groups or memberships include but are not limited to jobs, schools, boards, services, and charities. Once inside the group, a new member gains some protection, advantage, power, and authority. The organization gains a member but also potential vulnerability and liability. The vetting process is used to reduce vulnerability and liability to the organization or relationship when the new member gains access.

The very same dynamic occurs on a more personal and often an unconscious level when we seek friends and establish relationships. We naturally protect ourselves by not exposing our vulnerabilities until there is a benefit and some evidence that we won't be hurt. So a subtle testing goes on before we will allow ourselves to be vulnerable to somebody we bring into our circle, friends, group or network. Thus when somebody new comes to us and presents themselves to us, we will test or "get to know" that person. Once we determine that an applicant would benefit the relationship, we bring them into our association. Abe Lincoln wrote:

"We destroy an enemy when we make them our friend,"

And this is a strategy implemented naturally by our feelings intelligence.

Feeling accepted means that we have been given membership after some scrutiny. We are telling ourselves after expressing interest in joining a group or relationship; admission was approved. We were outside and now we're in.

There is no invitation for application or certification of acceptance that goes out to the one seeking the relationship. All of that is accomplished without formal interviews, massive paperwork, human resources departments, or burgeoning admissions bureaucracy. We give each other emotive signals, and we receive them back without conscious effort. That is because our wild elephant can speak with other wild elephants directly. If we hear the conversation between the wild elephants at all, we are "in tune." And when we feel accepted, we are telling ourselves that it's safe and beneficial that we travel together. Make it so.

Sexual Love

Pleasurable feelings make our lives fun, enjoyable, and worth living. They provide motivation by rewarding certain behavior and decisions. Sexual feelings provide motivation in relationships for coupling. The message of arousal is that the object of my desire can make me feel unbelievably wonderful, and life is fantastic when we are involved with this person. There is an urgency to drop other activities momentarily and choose this one.

Nature favors coupling; sexual love is the insurance that a species would survive. To insure survival, nature made sexual pleasure the most intense pleasure. In doing that, nature ensured individuals bonding for the purposes of procreation, family and living in groups. This works to increase survival chances over living as single individuals.

With many competing available options, lifestyles and choices, feelings of sexual love provide that extra motivation to couple for a family.

Preservation of lasting relationships result from pleasurable emotions. The message of sexual feeling is that staying together is mutually beneficial. The feeling of erotic love produces an intense desire to be with somebody. Sexual love's message is we are fulfilled, and complete in body, mind, and soul.

Sexual love's message is to share a common path. It is said life is short and we need a great travel companion. Sexual feelings bring individuals together very effectively, without resorting to sifting through piles of resumes or scrutinizing qualifications and pedigrees. Somehow we know who our ideal companion is when we feel sexual. The message of sexual feelings is we want to share some joy with this person.

Confidence

The feeling of confidence informs us of the degree of certainty or uncertainty that we have regarding a contemplated action or decision. Confidence is built from within by the memories of successful and unsuccessful activities that we have experienced or know about.

There are no guarantees in life. Time and chance is determinative in many activities successful conclusion. We all have a personal actuary of sorts. An actuary deals with risk and uncertainty; evaluates the likelihood of events and quantifies the contingent outcomes in order to minimize losses associated with uncertain undesirable events. Our actuary knows everything that we ever did and experienced. This actuary estimates what our chances for success are on any particular matter. This actuary lives inside of us as part of our emotional system. We know him as self-confidence. When you think about doing something, you will get a nod or not from this feeling, on you chances for success.

We use another's confidence in a similar way. We deal with people we don't know well, and sometimes we are called upon to make snap judgments about their abilities. One can always ask, "Have you done this before?" "What were the results?" "Do you have the experience to know what could go wrong and anticipate that?" or "What special skills do you have to do this correctly?" "Do you have formal training in this area?" and so forth. The appearance of confidence informs us that we can rely on other's to save ourselves the time, just by their confidence. But beware, con artists rely heavily on the appearance of confidence for the above-mentioned reason; we bank on another's apparent confidence without more testing.

Confidence is used early and shapes our path. Some children engage in competitive play, based on their confidence in winning or prevailing. If they do not feel confident that they can at least hold their own, they are not likely to let themselves into the game to suffer ridicule or certain failure.

We are designed to survive and therefore to win, to prevail. The higher the stakes, the more confidence we need to overcome the risk of loss. As our confidence builds, so can our skill and vice versa.

Confidence is your personal trainer that informs you that this is an activity at which you can excel, it's profitable, and you can succeed. Lack of or low confidence, informs you that you need more practice and homework. Degree of confidence will tell you how much more or what kind of practice you need to build up before you are ready to engage.

Before we take action we automatically check in with our confidence first. We may also determine that the time or resources are not sufficient to build the confidence to the level required, and then we have used our lack of confidence to make an intelligent decision not to engage.

Jim related to me that as a young adult, he worked a dangerous job, surface painting a bridge at dizzying heights. He had to force himself to work because the extreme fear induced in him uncontrollable shaking. But in three months time his confidence was so high, that he could scamper about hundreds of feet above certain death without much trepidation.

He reflected that this experience built confidence. Although not his first choice occupation, the confidence served Jim well in other areas. This should tell you that a confidence feeling is statistical in nature, that your chances of doing well at some activity can be related to doing well in another activity. The personal actuary inside you calculates the numerical complexity of the circumstance or situation, leaving you with a feeling of confidence or lack thereof for success.

Compassion

The feeling of compassion is a profound human emotion prompted by the pain of another. More vigorous than empathy, compassion commonly gives rise to an active desire to alleviate another's suffering.

Perception of another's pain leaves us with a desire to alleviate the pain. Pain and suffering can occur from myriad causes in many forms. Roughly half of our feelings are painful, but those from inside us. Compassion gives us the ability to detect pain external to ourselves. Our feeling of compassion identifies not only the external pain source, but also the extent of that pain and suffering.

Compassion implements a self-preservation strategy because when we ignore another's pain, we potentially hurt ourselves. We instinctually know, minus circumstance or happenstance, that another's pain can be ours. Perhaps we were lucky, and if we were in the other's person's shoes we would want help.

The Good Samaritan from scripture is the famous story about compassion. A traveler was robbed, and was left for dead by the thieves. A passing Samaritan felt compassion, and stopped at a dangerous road site to help and perhaps save the life of a complete stranger. A priest and a Levite, who saw the victim, did not stop, because their fear exceeded possible feelings of compassion.

Fear has a tendency to travel with compassion, because often we are vulnerable to the same fate as the suffering victim, if we render aid and assistance. Rendering aid and more, the Samaritan was viewed as a "neighbor" even though he was a complete stranger to the victim. That is the message of compassion – no matter what our race, religion or skin color, we are all neighbors and have a duty to render aid when we see another in pain. Compassion supersedes race, religion, and political affiliation because our natural strategy for survival is specie wide.

Without compassion, our ability to identify those in need of our help would be impaired. We are all limited beings with precious resources. Those resources can only be energized a finite number of times. Therefore, their allocation is important. Compassion tells us, to the extent that we are able, we need to help others in pain, because allocation of our precious resources is served well there.

Compassion is our external pain sensor. We feel less compassion for the rich and much compassion for the poor, because our feelings of compassion tell us where and when to render aid, and what form it should take. Deep down we know if circumstances were reversed and we needed help, a little help would go a long way.

Connectedness

Feeling connected is the precursor to meaningful communication, and therefore sound relationships. Before any vital or important communication can transpire, one must feel connected, or the feelings information in the communication will fail.

Two-way radio communicating follows a protocol to facilitate word or text transfer.

Communicating parties say "over" when they are finished speaking and "I copy" to acknowledge receipt of a communication. This is the protocol for verbal or textual communication where clarity is of vital import. In like fashion, we have a parallel protocol for feelings communication.

Because feelings carry the bulk of the important information, we need a way to understand when the transmitted feelings are received and acknowledged. Without a connection first, the communication will be broken, partial or non-functional; we can't get a feeling across the human-to-human chasm, and the message will be lost. Without the feeling of connection, we are building the tower of Babel, the sender is a random generator, and the receiver is burdened with ambiguity, decryption and misunderstanding.

One must first feel heard and validated, knowing that the communication will be understood at the level intended. Absent the feeling of connection, we are just exchanging words on a wire or a text stream in cyberspace.

The message of feeling connected tells you that everything you communicate thereafter will be understood, and carry the truth, value, depth, and weight that you intended. The communication will overcome any noise on the line or in the receiver. Protocol is common in communication and we have connectedness is built in for feelings transmission.

That's what connectedness does and that's why the feeling of connection needs to be established early in a communication. That is also why we greet each other with, "How are you?" Moreover, connection engages when it registers as sincere, that it matters. This is vital component that our wild elephant will sense.

Arguments ensue regularly when individuals, who do not first feel connected, attempt to communicate. These arguments can become heated and loud, not because the participants are hard of hearing, but because they don't feel connected, and they are attempting to overcome the invisible blockage with sound volume. Even if the volume is deafening, a disconnected individual will rightfully not "get it."

Alternately, the message of feeling disconnected is that you need to connect first. To connect, ask a person how they are feeling, make eye contact, and listen to them. Show them first you are ready to hear, to receive their words and feelings. For example, offer understanding for their concerns, validate their feelings, and applaud their efforts. That little protocol up front can invoke the connection feeling, and bridge the chasm. The feeling of being connected gives us the message that the line is clear, and now we can communicate at the depth required. George Eliot described this beautifully with:

"Oh the comfort, the inexpressible comfort of feeling safe with a person, having neither to weigh thoughts nor measure words, but pouring them all right out, just as they are -- chaff and grain together -- certain that a faithful hand will take and sift them, keep what is worth keeping, and with the breath of kindness blow the rest away."

Without the connection feeling, we simply talk at another. Feeling connected, we know even our whisper is heard, is validated, and carries the weight, value, truth, meaning, and at the volume intended. Connectedness is the essence of friendship.

Excitement

I took my son to see the movie "Toy Story" when he was six years old. Driving home, my son related how much he enjoyed the movie, but that he was particularly excited about a box helmet with wings, which one character wore. For the life of me I could **not** remember seeing the said helmet; I could remember no such helmet. But my little son described it in such vivid detail, so I believed he saw a helmet. I agreed to build it for him. I decided to see the movie a second time, just to make sure that I got the helmet design right.

Sure enough, my son was correct. But the entire helmet sequence was but a few fleeting seconds, and probably a prop most would miss. I did. In the movie the main human character, Andy's sadistic neighbor child, runs into his house, removes a box with eyeholes, and quickly discards it in the hall corner, all while running from outside the house to his bedroom. I forgot the scene, before I even saw it. I had to see the sequence several times. But my son saw it the first time, and it excited him so much, that his persistence and descriptive detail compelled me to build such a helmet out of a box. Only after I constructed the thing, did I see the "wings," the box flaps. My son said "the helmet had wings" and indeed it did. The excitement burned every detail into his memory, while it did not even singe mine.

To this day, I cannot fathom what great importance constructing a box helmet with eyeholes and wings for my son would accomplish, but I can see that feeling of excitement, burned a detailed imprint of something intriguing into his memories, and instantly persuaded me to stop dead in my tracks, and listen to a small child who directed me in a project. I doubt that he even remembers much about it now, but that experience was burned into my memory, as if it were yesterday.

Excitement tells you, "Don't deny this: it's important." Excitement anticipates and announces a significant moment even though sometimes it's not obvious or routinely accepted.

Excitement also has an infectious quality, whereby we can share a memorable moment in time with somebody. And this sharing results in a life-size payoff, a moment shared builds a bond, makes a connection, bridges, and transfers experience. Sometimes, excitement tells you that you are close to a goal or a finish line, informs you that attainment is within reach. Excitement reports all of that in an instant.

Inspiration

Inspiration drives the need for self-actualization, the very capstone in Maslow's Hierarchy. According to Maslow's Hierarchy of Needs, if you are in a survival mode, your needs will be occupied with physical survival and you are less likely to feel the luxury of inspiration. Nevertheless, I believe that inspiration can occur at any time, and is not limited to the fulfillment of other needs immediately prior.

This is because inspiration can also alleviate, reduce, and stave off hunger, tiredness, discomfort, and even physical pain. We are an infinitely inventive species and are limited by few boundaries; the farthest boundary is that of imagination. Inspiration crosses over that boundary to provide us with undiscovered territory.

However, from a practical matter, it is more difficult to feel inspired if you are experiencing great physical discomfort, starving, or freezing because your emotions are firing off intense signals telling you to survive the more immediate threat.

Inspiration leads also to ownership of a new idea or intellectual property, a contribution of exceptional value or work. This leads to achievement and legacy. Inspiration drives invention; it provides motivation to create novel products or business. We are at sentient synergistic beings, and much more than the sum of our parts. Inspiration leverages on that multiplier advantage from feelings, and transcends logic to arrive at a novel solution.

The reward of inspiration tells you that you can reach the peak, climb the mountain, that the view will take your breath away, stopped the beating of your heart for a split second. The cost you paid becomes irrelevant. We are programmed to succeed and through inspiration, we receive a positive reinforcement rush of pleasure.

The message of inspiration is that we are creators and that our contributions, once implemented, live on. Our prime directive is therefore fulfilled beyond our mortal self. And some would say enters the spiritual realm.

No writing on inspiration is complete without Edison's observation "Invention is 1% inspiration and 99% perspiration." Without inspiration, the overwhelming 99% of the effort could not have occurred. Inspiration gives us that kick-start at a precise time to send us on a creative mission that will task our behavior and thoughts, those trained elephants that are also part of us.

Inspiration occurs when the wild elephant gives the trained elephants, thinking and behavior, direct commands that they can understand, and energizes them to perform. This demonstrates the power of the wild elephant, that 1%, emotion, can direct 99% of your resources, thinking and behavior, to achieve a remarkable result; an achievement packed in a contribution.

Joyousness

Joy says celebrate your win; it was a strenuous test of your mettle, and the race was close. Joy is a celebration of life and achievement, extreme happiness. Why does nature bestow this gift? Joy is the message of the certainty of a life continued. You have achieved a lofty goal, and we re-enforce this for a repeat performance, or greater future achievements. Joy runs with glory, attainment culminated from intense feeling or thoughts.

Ecstasy is joy intensified. Some believe that "Life is hard then you die." And without joy and ecstasy in life, we may not feel life was worth the journey. But ultimately life always is, and so the feeling joy and ecstasy was provided to insure that we know that life is worth the good fight.

The feeling of joy can come in the form of exhilaration, produced by a chemical release from an intense situation wherein we survived a close call. Again, the message is thanks, positive reinforcement for great decisions and performance.

No discussion of ecstasy is complete without the mention of sexual relations. Joy and ecstasy are both indelibly embedded within. Without these immense motivators, joy and ecstasy, we as a species would not be as prolific or industrious. These feelings are the insurance that we survive as a species and grow in numbers, the fulfillment of our prime directive.

Loyalty

Everyday we are beset with choices, this product or that, this job or that, this service or that. The message of loyalty is "choose this one above that one." At times we must make quick decisions regarding products, services, groups, alliances. Knowledge or experiences with these will build the feeling of loyalty in us because absent knowledge or experience with the other options and insufficient time for research, we make quicker decisions going with what we know or have experienced even though we cannot recall specifics, because it's the statistically correct strategy.

The feeling of loyalty is easily confused with our duty of loyalty. We all have beliefs that we have a duty of loyalty to our country, family, partner, religion, ethnic group, but maybe not in that order. We often have a hierarchy of duties of loyalty and this often makes for interesting stories, where the hero suffers through conflicted loyalties. In the movie *2001 Space Odyssey*, HAL the life support controlling computer attempts to kill off the crew. We find out later this happens because HAL's programming had "conflicting priorities" provoking this schizophrenic behavior.

We can get very intense feelings of loyalty where the choice to be made is more personal or life threatening. The natural group instinct tells us that our survive and thrive chances are better when we favor the group we have history with or is closest to us. However, our feelings take from our present and past experience, not the future.

Marketers work hard to build brand loyalty. Much research shows this powerful way of affecting buy decisions. Marketers inundate us with advertisements knowing that we will eventually come to a decision point and seeing the brand will invoke all of the advertizing material in a feeling of loyalty. But reality is the great equalizer. This will be accounted for in our feeling of loyalty.

Passion

Passion is an intense compulsion or a strong

affinity or love towards a person, subject, idea or object. Conventional wisdom teaches passion is an emotion that needs to be controlled. "Rule your passions or your passion will rule you," is the adage.

But the message of passion is not to be subdued. The message of passion is first spend time and energy with this idea, pursuit, or person. The second is to change your priorities, go for it, and don't look back.

When passion strikes we are telling ourselves, "I don't know how I know, I just know that I need to do or be this." Passion brings energy, excitement, and enthusiasm to help you achieve a remarkable result. Regarding the emotion of passion, Henri Amiel wrote in 1856:

> "Without passion man is a mere latent force and possibility, like the flint which awaits the shock of the iron before it can give forth its spark."

Inventors, artists, and creative people in all walks of life are frequently gifted with passion, as they need to tune out so much noise to focus on their creations. Listen to the message and follow your passion. Passion tells us to focus on the object of our passion. We are telling ourselves we have found our way.

Optimism

Optimism informs us to put the most favorable construction upon actions and events or to anticipate the best possible outcome. Optimists generally believe that people are inherently good and events generally happen for good reasons, so that most situations conclude for the best. This is an attitude or behavior pattern and not the feeling.

The message of optimism is to continue our efforts that we will prevail and meet with success. This is a powerful feeling when you are faced with imperfect or conflicting information. The factual answer or solution is not apparent, but the feeling of optimism says that you have some evidence, knowledge, or wisdom within, which substantiates that you will survive and prevail.

We absorb prodigious quantities of information, and subconsciously or consciously construct possible outcomes in overcoming challenges. Our thinking hinges on models or scenarios we create to predict or explain behavior and futures. As such, depending on the scenarios and models we chose, we can predict either a negative or a positive outcome.

Optimism is the feeling that tells us to use the models or scenarios to project positive outcomes, because something in our knowledge or experience substantiates a positive outcome. And some of us are blessed with a more optimistic nurture or nature than others. Optimism provides the energy to fulfill the prophecy it is making.

Peacefulness

"I get a peaceful easy feeling, 'cause I'm already standing on the ground," lyrics from an

Eagle's song seem to resonate, when I think about a peaceful feeling. "I want to sleep with you in the desert tonight," actually suggests another feeling, never the less, the song has been burned into my easy access memory associated with the words peaceful feeling.

There is confusion regarding this emotion. That confusion is between states of peace, generally a political, societal, or cultural goal, and the feeling of peace, which is a very relaxed feeling we sometimes have. Nothing against world peace, I think it's a great idea, but feeling peaceful is about lack of feeling stressed and very personal. The peaceful feeling can occur no matter what the state of the world is or isn't, unless of course your neighborhood or country is at war.

When feelings are not triggered, our feelings disposition or mood stays near neutral, the peaceful feeling comes when your physical, psychological, and emotional states are all near equilibrium. Some religious teachings practice the attainment of the peaceful feeling through meditation and other behavioral means as part of a life purpose or goal.

When you get the stressed-out or emotionally or mentally drained feeling, you need psychological and emotional rest until you feel the peaceful feeling. Then you know your emotive and mental resources are repaired and recharged. That is the message of the peaceful feeling, that you are completely recharged and fully ready to continue your journey.

When we override, ignore or don't know what to do with our stressful or overwhelmed emotions, we can continue to get run down until we suffer a nervous, mental or emotional breakdown or disorder.

You had better find that peaceful easy feeling before you have to pull over or get into a figurative accident. Do what it takes to get your peaceful feeling back. Peaceful is a wonderful feeling to have because it indicates adventure is just ahead, you're heading back on the road. You're good-to-go.

Trust

Who should I trust? When should I trust? Where should I put my trust and in what should I trust? The answer lies within, within you.

Trust is that emotion that you get when you feel that pleasure of letting go of an issue, and worry does not arise.

We are constantly being sold trust in things, concepts, structures, ideas, and people some of which are good for us, and others, which are not. And much that we are sold is what we do not truly need or want. But, the more that we cognitively know about a matter, the more difficult it is to be persuaded to trust in a matter, as we have more data brings more issues.

Sometimes we just don't know what we know, at least on a conscious thinking level, or we may have imperfect information. This is where the feeling of trust pays dividends. But to be useful, trust requires honesty with ourselves, because trust comes from within, but only when we let go of something.

To have trust in a matter requires that we have some knowledge or experience. Lacking information, we will receive natural feelings of caution, distrust, fear, doubt, or disbelief.

But trust informs us that we have reason to believe that the matter is as we understand it to be from a deeper than conscious level, and those reasons are substantiated by something that we know or have experienced, but don't need to recall at the moment. In his poem 'If' Rudyard Kipling writes:

"If you can trust yourself when all men doubt you, but make allowance for their doubting too..."

Trust is based on your knowledge, experience, and understanding which may be considerable or not. But, if we accepted the message of trust, created options testing the trusted object commensurate with that level of trust we felt and relied on that decision, then we adequately addressed the trust message. That is the feelings intelligence was applied.

A Universal Language

Intelligent decisions are never easy decisions, and quite often arrive on the edge between trust and doubt, certainty and uncertainty. Discernment and introspection will require that we be a feelings prospector, and truly mine for trust to determine what it is that we feel.

Elephant is a universal language that uses words, sounds, and gestures as vehicles to convey information and meaning. As such, often times the words or sounds will be ancillary, ambiguous, and interchangeable. The language of emotions transcends the vehicles used in communication. I have found that communication rich in feelings are more persuasive than just thoughts, as they are nearer to truth we know and carry a resonating component more deeply understood. We inherently know truth through our feelings. Learning the language of Elephant is simple, but quicker through immersion.

5 – Guests Bring Needs

All needs, wants and desires are born from and borne by feelings. When we get hungry, it follows that we need food. When we feel cold; we need to find warmth, clothing, and or shelter. When we feel lonely, we need companionship; we need to talk to somebody. Curious? We need to search, or research and you need to understand the object of your curiosity.

When we have a feeling we frequently have a need, but the feeling is the trigger. It's a simple almost cause-effect mapping from feelings to needs. It's our wild elephant warning us of the road up ahead. We let ourselves know when we need something and when we need to start developing options to fill a future need to insure our survival and thrival.

Of course, our cognitive self, the thinking mind, our trained elephant, can override our needs signals to a degree. Our thinking mind can find a substitute, or distract us altogether – override the feelings message. That is frequently the case and is often done out of denial, procrastination, or ignorance – the three horsemen of indecision. That's when we don't see the signal and throw away

Feelings ignored are issues not addressed, are decisions delayed, and are needs unmet. Our needs do not cease unless they are satisfied and the trigger feeling issue resolved. If we have a feeling doing nothing about it amounts to indecision, which is usually the wrong decision as it ignores the message. That message we are giving ourselves because we need to know it in that instant and not another.

Feelings drive needs and needs drive decisions. But knowing feelings has other advantages over knowing needs. Knowing present needs only gets us so far because these only reach what we consciously know. But we ultimately need to fulfill an emotion, or solve an issue. That decisions are emotionally based is well known because emotions point to real issues and what we will need in the future. Thus the search for need fulfillment can be anticipatory or pre-emptive, if we address the feelings message in fulfillment options. Otherwise our search for fulfillment is doomed because we think we need something until we acquire it, and then discover that didn't resolve the underlying feeling. There is an effectiveness and efficiency to feelings fulfillment that can be lost on need fulfillment because feelings are anticipatory of needs and needs tend to be perceived when we don't address the underlying message.

Insight into Others

This brings us to a very important point – that knowing another's feelings gives us insight into their currently governing issues and their real needs, just as knowing our feelings brings about the conscious awareness of our own needs and desires. Without a careful understanding of another's emotional states,

116

we cannot think our way to the correct need or solution for them. Our interaction, service, or product will not be wholly beneficial, complete, or fulfilling to them. Hence our friend, patient, client, or customer will not receive the things that they need or want, and we will have done less than we could have in our service. Thus intuition, thoughtful observation, careful attention to detail, active listening, and psychological insight means that we need to zero in on the other's feelings, and deal with the messages and issues given them to guide us to what is truly needed and wanted for them.

Feelings are how we figure out what is in our best interest and also what is in another's best interest. Ultimately, we consult our feelings for decisions because that is most efficient. Those that are feelings aware are always the quickest to true fulfillment.

Crossed Signals

Some teach that our feelings are triggers to actions. That is not the case. Thinking is what determines actions. We can think of many solutions for a given triggered feeling and even partial solutions. Acting on partial solutions tends to give us some relief and sometimes the illusion that we are done, feeling fulfilled and issue resolved. At times, our thinking is so ingrained or automatic, much though is not required and we don't realize that time was spent thinking up our response expression or action because we engaged an automatic rule, a heuristic. Habits and beliefs are thinking aids that we use to automate good decisions which can be made in advance.

But at times quick response action to a feeling is necessary for our survival. This is as basic as the decision for fight or flight. Is the signal anger or fear respectively? We must make the correct feeling identification in an instant by plotting our course from issue to the best possible future.

Our process must be correctly threaded, other wise we suffer from poor decisions which lead to implementation of inadequate solutions and those lead to bad or wrongful behavior. Action without regard to the triggering feeling message is a major cause of error and consequent misbehavior. For our solution to be true we must address the feeling message and apply that message to the correct object of the feeling, end-to-end.

Deep seated or intense emotions affect our judgments. That is also by design. Strong feelings are high priority messages from ourselves telling us what is most important and consequently what is of lesser import. Therefore addressing feeling messages with weight from feelings intensity, provide us with additional information for our discernment and judgment. Addressing our feeling's intensity serves to enhance the power of our judgments adding timeliness.

We are multi-tasking creatures, handling many external and internal events and with variable urgencies virtually simultaneously. And therein lies the potential for crossed signals. Letting intense feelings on a matter "bleed" into our judgments on an unrelated matter is where the crossed signals cause misjudgments or exercise of poor judgment.

Therefore we must take care to ascertain the trigger feeling, associate that feeling message with the object of the feelings, and ascertain that the decision we are making resolves the trigger feeling we experienced. Keeping a tight couple between feelings and judgments reduces the likelihood that our chosen solutions and actions will be inappropriate or just plain wrong. Often it is not the solution that saves us, but the absence of mistakes.

In terms of speed, our emotions are light years faster than our thinking. Hence, without emotions our automatic access to our experiential knowledge base is not timely, and may cost more than we planned for or can imagine. Another characteristic of emotions is that they are always timely, as we receive feelings from ourselves at precisely the moment that we need them. But in resolving a feeling, we can trigger other feelings. The world does not wait and nature insured that we be responsive. It's the quick and the dead. If we feel overwhelmed, we are informing ourselves that our feelings system is overloaded. The message of feeling overwhelmed is seek a less dynamic environment, one that can be confidently managed in the moment. To ignore that message risks crossed signals and judgment impairment.

Because our survival depends on it, feelings do not wait on thought completions, they are spontaneous and asynchronous. We may get a feeling in the middle of a thought. It's best to hold the though and address the feeling, as it may have a bearing on the thoughts exercised. Our wild elephant hears our thoughts and interrupts our thinking when

119

we know something important needs to be factored into our cognitive deliberations.

Without emotions, our ability to make decisions is limited to our serial one-thought-at-a-time conscious brain, too slow and clunky to handle real-time issues or complex problems. Emotions are our tool for efficient navigation in the unchartered darkness of space-time in what's typically called our future, where one must respond quickly and correctly or spin thrusters frantically trying to think a way out.

At times we get a feeling and we are off on a fools errand thinking we know how to respond, we have built in automatic defaults. This is when we need to remember also that the feelings intensity, the other vital component to the signal, gives us additional information about the priority, weight or urgency associated with our response. Did we respond to quickly to a low intensity feeling, or did we not respond quickly to a high intensity feeling? Did we execute on an intense feeling and let a lesser intensity feeling slide off unaddressed? Let your feelings intensity meter your judgment, but don't forget we can have more than one feeling, and they all need to be addressed without fail, or our solution will.

The 2008 Banking Failure Bailout is a good example. People felt angry about helping the wealthy Wall Street bankers out of the financial mess that they created for themselves, their investors and the economy. But we were told by almost everyone that we trusted, that if we didn't help Wall Street, then we would soon be chasing after rat meat in the streets.

Fear was used in a concerted mass media blitz to approve the bailout. The average persons fear was driven to a level where the anger was not registering or addressed. Consequently, the Wall Street received the bail out that they lobbied for, and then moved quickly to neutralize any real efforts at regulation. Then celebrating their mission accomplished by issuing themselves bonuses for a job well done. Meanwhile, the further sliding jobless economy was driving fear into most of us, and we felt helpless to do anything about our anger. Thus we ignored our feelings of *anger* and *helplessness*, but addressed our *fear*, as it was so intense. Like all mistakes in not addressing our feelings, good decisions are precluded. Remedies are only band-aids and illusory at best. The root cause will always come back again and again to cause more pain. The instability will increase each cycle; until nature imposes a remedy we generally call a "disaster nobody could have prevented." Our feelings were are right and true, but when we fail to address all of them fully, we don't address our needs faithfully. This is the death of feelings intelligence.

6 – Entertaining Guests, Processing

In order to be a good host, we must process our feelings starting with the practice of mindfulness, a detached observing mind introspecting our feelings on a particular matter. Practicing mindfulness means we graciously invite our guests in, receive their message and the associated message issue into our thoughts. Remember that an unaddressed feeling, not letting our guest in to the party, only delays a decision, builds up stress and increases our risk to something known. To know what our feelings are telling us, our thinking mind must process thoughts associated with the identified feeling's message and then the impinging issue. The emotion's messages are therefore our translation toolkit that magnifies or increases the radius of our cognitive awareness. We need to look for the information surrounding the feelings issue. Resolve and move on, we have entertained our guest. Our awareness increases when we read our feelings and use the message of the feeling to direct resolution of the associated issue.

Feel-Think-Act

Although multiple feelings may trigger almost simultaneously, thinking is a predominantly serial step-by-step process. Learning should start simple. Therefore reception and handling of a feeling is step one. The following is the step-by-step ready-aim-fire process on how to apply feelings to obtain powerful results:

1) When we feel something, and at times it can be very subtle, take ownership, it's really us. Our feelings are trying to inform our thinking mind regarding a matter of import. If we recognize another's feeling, we need to make a mental note of the external source, and not confuse them with our own feelings. Processing is analogous to our internal source feeling.

2) Identify the feeling. It has a name: Is it anger, fear, hate, frustration, anxiety, boredom, resentment? Where more than one feeling, name them all.

3) Acknowledge that we received the message and thank yourself. I know how strange that sounds, but it tells your guest that he's welcome, that we received the message and in that pause we reload our calm thinking mind with the new challenge.

4) Ask yourself: What is this feeling telling me? Or: What is the message of this feeling?

5) Now engage your cognitive mind, your thinking elephant, and let him figure out what action to take. First, find the specific object of the message. For example, in the message of hate, tells us to get some distance between us and the hated, until we gain understanding. The hated is the object of our hate.

6) Craft solutions that address the feelings message and its true object, and be as crafty as you can be. With the hate example, maintain or increase your distance, minimize potential for interaction, always have a third party around, try to understand the hated's position, review your own understanding and beliefs – What are they? How did you come by them? What is their basis or foundation?

7) Choose one or more solutions you crafted to act on. Ascertain that it addresses the feeling and true object of the emotion's message. It may seem like you are angry with somebody, but you may really be angry at what that person represents e.g. the unfairness of law, not the law enforcement officer, the unfairness of the culture or economics, not the business prices. Hone into the issue object and be as precise as you can be.

8) If you still feel the emotion after implementing your resolving expression, your action did not resolve the issue, and the feeling will lodge and wait until it is resolved You are informing yourself that the impending issue still exits. General problems have very large solution sets. Precision here narrows the solution to specifics and more appropriate to an implementable solution. At times just acknowledging that you received the feeling's message with your conscious thoughts will allow yourself to feel the calm, as you picture the resolution. If not, try your next solution. Resolution is the feedback loop for each feeling.

Check to see:

- **Anger** subsides when fairness is restored.
- **Fear** retreats when you take proper precautions.
- **Hate** dissolves when you get distance and understanding.
- **Frustration** disappears when you get more time. Or attain your goal another way.
- **Anxiety** is reduced when you practice and prepare.
- **Boredom** disappears when you change venue.
- **Resentment** dissipates when you reallocate your efforts.
- **Humiliation** preserves you, when you retreat and take stock.

This process absolutely requires that you use or develop introspection and listening skills. There is nothing like practice. Being introspective pays dividends. When you have a feeling, ask yourself, "What am I feeling? What is the message of that feeling?" Having lists of feelings and reminders of messages mapped to feelings is also helpful.

Repeated consultation with our feelings makes us more aware, alert, smarter, and more powerful because we are using more of our knowledge and experience to address the most relevant issue facing us in the moment. We are working smarter by not wastefully disregarding those messages from the wild free elephant within, our emotive force.

What emotions give us is raw intelligence. The intensity of the emotion informs us how we need to prioritize the issue that we face.

Fight or flight is the action, triggered from the emotions of anger or fear, respectively. The decision for action can be made in an instant, but feelings are the precursors, the signals that point us to the issue – unfairness or danger, respectively. Even though our technology and civilization has improved our lives dramatically, our survival and thrival still always depend on our feelings to guide us.

Some individuals seem to lead a charmed life. We meet them and we know they are different, special. They have that touch, that quality. Some explain it by good karma and some explain it by time and chance – they are just lucky.

My explanation is that those individuals are very feelings aware and apply excellent feelings intelligence, which provides a superior foundation for their thinking and behavior, a calm and a harmony in their lives regardless of the circumstances. They know their feelings are friends, informing them of things that they need to consider and take care of in the moment. And that it gives them their best shot. They manage their lives well and makes them successful in life.

When we resolve our emotions and our needs are satisfied, we are able to worry and be happy, fear the unsafe, and hate our way to love. That's where resolution leads, and we need not stop until we get to our destination if we pack right.

7 – Your Neighbor's Guest House

From time to time it's useful to know our friends, enemies, relatives, neighbors, customers or client's needs. Maslow's hierarchy of needs is still one of the most used principles in business and psychology. Maslow's hierarchy rests on a progression or priority of needs, with fulfillment of lower or baser needs precluding the higher needs from occurring prior to the lower need fulfillment. This hierarchy is generally depicted as forming a solid stable pyramid structure of a human's prioritized list of very general needs. In some fields, our needs define us. We become what we eat, where we shop and what we do to fill those needs. Hence the Maslow hierarchy is used to identify market segments by habits, lifestyles and demographics, but ultimately based on our needs; perceived, generated or real.

Advertisers use needs and wants to target a particular demographic, a fancy word for a range of income, wealth, age, or skin color. A particular product or service fills a need better for the target group because of where they fall on the physical, social, or personal Maslow needs hierarchy layer. But this apparent solid pyramid of needs rests on a very dynamic bed of emotions. But at best this approach targets groups, not individuals. It's a one size fits all strategy. However, to address individuals instead of groups, one must first be able to capture a feeling.

As we know, feelings are the precursors to needs which drive decisions. That decisions are emotionally based is well known. Knowing needs will only get you so far, because needs only reach what you consciously think you require, and this may differ from fulfilling an emotion or resolving an issue. Emotions point to what we need or will need; thus they are predictive and anticipatory. The search for need fulfillment therefore, need not be a conscious thinking burden since a known feeling anticipates a need. Thus knowing feelings is of great value because matching needs with need fulfillment can be anticipated by matching feelings with issue resolution.

A very persuasive and personable sales person, Stan, once lamented that he made a really big deal with a client, but they only had a verbal agreement and the client was going on vacation. After the client came back from vacation, he rescinded the agreement. Stan said, "I knew that was going to happen." I asked him how he knew.

Stan said, and this is something that good sales people are skilled in knowing, that that for large deals that carries significant risk, there is always buyer's remorse. It was natural that the deal would unravel during the vacation, because vacations are not when we handle risk issues very well. Vacations are when we want to relax; recharge, and we cannot do that unless we unload feelings that give us stress, pain feelings. Remorse and regret are painful feelings, and our wild elephant never forgets because there is no beneficial vacation with pains outstanding.

So to come back refreshed and rested from vacation, we know deep down that we need to unload the pain. Hence the potential client's answer was predictably rescission, in order to relax and recharge, the potential client needed to eliminate his painful feelings. A decision to rescind a risky business deal made the pain from remorse go away, client's issue resolved.

As a sales person knowing that the customer may have regrets, the feeling that tells us that perhaps we made a mistake, we should handle that feeling issue then, and not wait for the wrong result to arrive as we know it inevitably will. Stan could have said, "Lets not make any decision now, relax and let's talk after you come back from your vacation." Thus he could have suggested postponing the decision so his client could have a relaxing vacation. Alternatively, Stan could have addressed the remorse feeling issue before the vacation and closed the deal then. His client would not have been tormented on his vacation.

Knowing that certain issues tend to trigger certain feelings in others helps us conduct our best strategy. There is a real practical side to feelings intelligence and the opportunities are those guests, knocking at your door. "Meet them at the door laughing, and invite them in." And don't forget the guests knocking at your customer's door; if we look and inquire, we can see them too.

This brings us to a very important point, that knowing another's feelings give us that insight into their governing issues and their real needs, just like they do with our own. Without a careful understanding of another's emotional state, we cannot think our way to the correct need or solution for them. Our product, service or interaction will not be beneficial, complete or fulfilling, unless it is responsive our clients feelings and issues. Hence our client, customer or patient will not be given the things that they need and we will have provided a lesser service or product.

Thus intuition, careful attention to detail, active listening, and psychological insight means that we need to zero in on the other's feelings, and deal with the messages and issues given to us in the moment, to help us respond to what is truly needed presently and in the future.

The open market economy works by the Adam's invisible hand, goes the metaphor. That is, people will trade based on only their own self-interests to guide them. Feelings are how we figure out what is in our best interests. Ultimately, consumers consult their feelings for purchase decisions because that is natural and most efficient. Therefore the feelings aware are always the quickest to fulfillment.

Professional life can certainly use the feelings power advantage. Dr. Peabody of Harvard Medical School in 1925 stated, "The secret of the care of the patient is in caring for the patient." But many doctors are taught to suppress their emotions, to block out natural reactions to the difficult treatments, and operations that they must perform. Some professionals believe that if they feel their emotions too deeply, they will not be objective, recoil or personally breakdown. But if they don't feel for their clients, they can fail in their care for them. Dr. Jerome Groopman, writes in *How Doctors Think*:

> "Cognition and emotion are inseparable. The two mix in every encounter with every patient... But a growing body of research show, technical errors account for only a small fraction of our incorrect diagnoses and treatments. Most errors are mistakes in thinking. And part of what causes these cognitive errors is our inner feelings, feelings we do not readily admit to and often don't even recognize."

This is a profound admission, that as professionals we don't know what to do about feelings, and when we do, the results are astounding. Currently, professionals, and I'm not speaking of only doctors, must struggle not only with their clients feelings but their own feelings as well. They struggle because they don't know what their feelings are telling themselves.

When feelings are in conflict and the issues unresolved, a lesser service is rendered. Hence professionals that do not clearly understand what the client's feelings are telling him, and unaware of his own feelings are at a double disadvantage. Both sets of feelings are incredibly rich information streams. The information is from the deepest recesses of knowledge, relevant, and sometimes absolutely critical. If the source of the emotions is the patient or client, then that is the source of the patient's issues. Caring for the patient is then addressing the patient's true issues and responding to those in conjunction with leveraging our own feelings which are based on

133

our knowledge and expertise. Recognizing and processing our feelings brings our expertise into the present and amplifies our power as professionals.

8 – Guest House Construction

Why can't we access all of our knowledge and experiences by recollection, when we need them? This is actually the key challenge that our brain solves. We cannot think fast enough to access our memory stores to find the pertinent information in a timely manner through our thinking mind. The simple truth is we have way too much memory and a relatively slow neuro-electrical process to access all of our memories with our cognitive thinking brain.

While the number of neurons in the human brain has been identified in cognitive and neural sciences, the magnitude of human memory capacity is still unknown. Some scientists believe that the memory capacity of the human brain, is on the order of 10^{8432} bits. That would be a "1" with 8,432 zeros after it. In comparison, our fastest computers only have terabytes of memory at most, which is a "1" with 12 zeros after it. Even accessing only a terabyte of memory is a significant challenge using the ever-popular computer von Neumann architecture, serial, sequential execution, a clunky one step at a time. If everybody in the world had a computer with a terabyte of data, all of the computer memory in the world would only amount to a "1" with 22 zero's after it.

The amount of memory capacity each one of us must manage is remarkably unbelievably and extraordinarily enormous. Accessing all of our memory is impossible by any technology that we have or will have for some time. But we all do it through feelings in real-time everyday without a conscious care.

Memory access algorithms are fast and becoming faster with hardware and software. But they are still so primitive compared to our massively parallel processing brain. For the computer scientist among us, I proffer that nature solved the equal latency for a growing memory tree with feelings, using a massive parallel processing scheme that undergoes load balancing at night. We call it dreaming.

For us technoids, we have a two architecture hybrid mind, thinking and feeling. The thinking, R-brain, uses a serial sequential step-by-step fetch and execute von Neumann architecture, which implements electrical impulses traversing our neural net. Our feelings, X-brain, use a massive parallel processor, at least part of which is chemical or fluidic memory which continuously and systematically accepts our entire sensor array, long term memories and biochemical inputs. These are filtered, multiplexed and loaded into our feelings registers accessible to our thinking mind. Where the signal is intense our thinking is interrupted immediately. When the feeling signal intensity is relatively low, we must introspect, poll, to acquire the resultant feeling.

We receive information from our biochemical processes – from hormones, pheromones, endorphins, adrenaline, neuro-transmitters, and more. And we receive data from our sensors and senses, five to nine, depending on whom you believe. These comprise our knowledge and memories. As you can understand, getting the data that you need when you need becomes a search, access and retrieve challenge. Again, this is an information bottleneck that our brain solves, the solution to accessing our data stores. This comprises our feelings architecture and we call it our emotional makeup upon instantiation starting even before birth. Feelings work in a massive parallel processor design, perhaps mostly chemical, but they work well and without any conscious thinking effort. This can be analogized to a direct memory access with prioritized queues. Nature provided immense processing power so that we could survive alone and thrive as a species together.

Specific memory improvement can also be exploited through the use of feelings. Lucas and Lorayne in their *The Memory Book* teach memory enhancement techniques that apply their principle that the more bizarre a specific memory, the easier to recall it. This is very effective and their techniques work very well applying these methods, associating bizarre images of peg words with objects to remember, later recalling the bizarre images to access the memory object. My theory as to why that is so, is that the more bizarre the memory, the more intense the feeling associated with storing that memory, and therefore the easier it is to access that memory object. Memory access speed and quality are functions of feeling intensity at storage time.

Albert Einstein said, "Imagination is more important than knowledge." Imagination comes from inspiration, a feeling, and knowledge comes from thinking. We have both. We need both. Use both. We should know how they work together if we are to survive and thrive as a species.

9 - A Guide From Inside, Go by Feel

Many psychologists, mental health professionals, and spiritual groups admonish us to live or "be in the moment." My initial response to that in the past was, as much as I'd like to live in the past or future, I'm stuck in the present, this moment. What choice do I have? Yes, I live in the moment, been doing that before you came along and told me. My understanding has changed.

What I've learned is that addressing our feelings in every moment is "being in the moment." We get notice and we can converse with ourselves through our feelings. At times we will feel something, but we are too busy. That is our bad training kicking in and we need to retrain ourselves to listen and trust that our feelings are true. Trust that our wild elephant only talks to us when we need to hear it. If we walk away from our feelings, we are shutting down one of the most vital parts of ourselves, we are saying NO to very relevant and timely information that we are at times urgently or sometimes very gently giving ourselves in the moment and by design.

Some studies indicate that we are not very good at identifying or recognizing our feelings. Therefore some argue that nothing practical can ever result from trying to use feelings, because we cannot even know what they are. But those studies failed to study people who were healthy and trained to be introspective, mindful, and trained to listen, address, and mine their feelings for information. We can learn to listen to our wild elephant and appreciate the message just like other personal skills.

Many religions and spiritual groups promote and promulgate the rules to achieve happiness or to find the secret to happiness. Those teachings can provide purpose or become our quest or obsession.

Many claim that life's quest begins with being at peace or they teach how to be at peace. The mantra quickly becomes, "Peace," "Peace now," "Got peace?" "Get peace," "Make peace with the moment," and many other catchy, touching, and ethereal slogans.

Some of the teachings in those books are beautifully written, flowery, but the words quickly dissolve into a verbal Rorschach. We soon see what we very much desire to see, believe what we much want to believe. But the reality is still a Rorschach.

I have not peppered you with beautiful prose, to ease your voyage. Our message is simple: pack light, take only what you need, what you can rely on, get there safe, be kind, and enjoy the ride.

Feelings – Rule of Thumb

As a review, I have listed the simple basic rule-of-thumb heuristics. A hallmark of feelings is that they are timely, effective, and efficient, providing vital information retrieval and issue prioritization. Our feelings help facilitate sound decision-making and intelligent communication.

All Feelings are Positive

There are no such things as negative feelings. Emotions are all signals, drawn, and benefiting from all of our knowledge and experience, residing in our memories and immediate sensory data, which in a timely manner gives us the sum total of all that information encapsulated in a feeling. Our decisions, behavior, or actions can be positive or negative, good or bad, but our feelings inform us from all that we are and all we know, through a resultant total feeling per issue bearing on something we immediately face or should consider for our future. The universe of events is too immense so our feelings give us the direction to look and which events are important to us. We are also informed of the intensity, the weight or gravity we should give that feeling issue. Focused effective thinking requires timely things to ponder. Action follows thinking. Conversely, action without feelings is random and weak. Action, as a result of feelings, is wisdom wrapped in common sense because it incorporates so much more of our knowledge and experience in the moment that it is most useful to us.

Emotive Lineup Rule

Sometimes we get that "funny" feeling and it gently nags or even bothers us. It's hard to identify and we naturally want to ponder it for a bit. It could be more than one feeling, so handle them one by one. Identify the feeling, it has a name; fear, despair, hope. The name or emotive state will tell you what is the valence: pleasure or pain. Feelings carry degrees of pleasure or pain, which, depending on the intensity, cry out for proportional action, but the underlying issue must be understood first, and the state identifier is the arrow that points at the issue or problem.

We are all a Standard Unto Ourselves

Most have seen judges grading divers, women assigning metrics to a man's sex appeal, men grading women, and generally a 10 scale is used. What we are doing is normalizing the intensity of our feeling on a scale of 1 to 10; with 1 being the least intense we have felt that feeling and 10 being the most intense. We do this so that we can combine with other's judgments. Where does this one lie? The intensity will quantify the emotional energy in the signal in a standard package, which is related to urgency, priority, relative importance, potential consequences standardized to us. Intensity is related to the energy we have invested in the matter. The intensity is also ultimately related to the subjective degree of the pleasure or pain that can be compared with concurrent feelings, since all of our feelings serial or concurrent can be mapped to a region of pleasure-pain space. Concurrent feelings can therefore add to or offset each other in this space and work together to give us our best over all option.

Feelings Traveling In Packs

At times near simultaneous feeling leave us with mixed feelings about a matter. We are complicated multitasking creatures dealing with many events, internal and external, occurring nearly simultaneously. For this reason feelings frequently travel in a packs or bunches. Take one feeling at a time; evaluate the message issue and object, group like objects, one-by-one. Most problems are complex, with many variables and many issues and options. Each feeling will address one or more issues and allow for at least several options. Take them apart, find the issues, weight them, order them, and add them up. That's our gut feel. So when our emotions come in a pack, divide and conquer. This commonality allows us to organize and deal with feelings uncoupled, independent of each other and yet put them altogether for the final analysis.

The CSI of Emotions

But who are we, who, who? In the popular CSI TV series, forensics experts are busy looking at clues, in order to solve the mystery of the victim's identity, post mortem, and externally. By that time it's too late for the victim.

The philosopher Rene Descartes admonished us to know ourselves. He wrote as if it were so very necessary and very difficult to attain, even wrapped in mystery and hardship. But it is necessary to know ourselves if we are to harness all of the power that lies within us. Not just your impulse engines, but our full power, quantum slip stream engine.

This can be very difficult because of all the misinformation that has been shoved into us without our authorization. This inhibits and retards our understanding and thus slows our vessel down. Knowing what our feelings are telling us can reduce the baggage, engage our full power, that wild elephant in us, and it will be an exuberant ride.

Some use their emotions perfectly, just by paying attention to what they feel, faithfully addressing the feelings, and enjoying the journey. The most difficult parts of our journey are riddled with clear sign posts from ourselves.

So, who are you? My answer for me – I am a sum of all of my experiences, memories, acts, behavior, physiological systems, physical attributes, talents, and skills. These are all stored inside me in various ingenious and incomprehensible ways.

The most obvious miracle is memory. We don't know how it works physically, but nature has given us amazing storage capacity at densities we cannot match with our highest technologies. The mysterious biochemical processes, which carry information internally, but how do they operate and communicate? There are trillions upon trillions upon trillions of terabytes of information that we all possess in memory, much of which is nearly impossible to retrieve without the side door access of hypnosis or dreams.

Much of that information and experience comes to us through our senses, and is not consciously registered, but it is yet stored somewhere and somehow within us. Multiply that by the myriad biochemical processes at work in our physical bodies, divide that by the smallest sensation from any of our 5 to 9 senses, depending on who you ask, and how they define a sense, that is the starting number of possibilities that we have. Those possibilities drive us to feel, think, act, and react in expression and behavior. These are all the components that comprise us, defining who we are.

Our feelings intelligence is what makes us the dominant specie on the planet, because it provides the power for us to be at our very best, when situations and circumstances are at their very worst. With our internal guidance system we can find that proverbial fork in the road and then choose to take path that makes all the difference. So if you think something is impossible, you're thinking too much – go by feel.

Bibliography

1. *Man's Search for Meaning,* Viktor E. Frankl

2. *The Memory Book*, Jerry Lucas and Harry Lorayne

3. *Anthony Robbins Power Emotions*!, http://www.youtube.com/watch?v=ahAgEUowGyQ

4. *How Doctors Think.* Dr. Jerome Groopman

About the Author

Walt Froloff is a recovering engineer, physicist, inventor, and practicing attorney residing in Northern California. He holds patents in the fields of Artificial Intelligence, Business Intelligence, Intelligent Engines, Air Hybrid Engine, Air Impulse Engine, and Consumer Products.

He has written *Irrational Intelligence,* the precursor to this book. His mantra is, "If you think it's impossible, you're thinking to much – go by feel."

More about how to harness the power of feelings intelligence in electronic devices can be found at www.FeelingsIntel.com.